ROMAN

ROMANO LAVO-LIL
WORD-BOOK OF THE ROMANY
OR, ENGLISH GYPSY LANGUAGE

BY GEORGE BORROW

WITH SPECIMENS OF GYPSY POETRY, AND AN
ACCOUNT OF CERTAIN GYPSYRIES OR
PLACES INHABITED BY THEM, AND
OF VARIOUS THINGS RELATING TO
GYPSY LIFE IN ENGLAND

ALAN
SUTTON
1982

Alan Sutton Publishing Limited
17a Brunswick Road
Gloucester

First published 1874

Copyright © in this edition 1982
Alan Sutton Publishing Limited

British Library Cataloguing in Publication Data

Borrow, George
  Romano Lavo-Lil.
  1. Gipsies — Great Britain
  I. Title
  941'.00491497   DX211

  ISBN 0-86299-024-6

Typesetting and origination by
Alan Sutton Publishing Limited.
Photoset Imprint 10/11
Printed in Great Britain
by Page Bros (Norwich) Limited.

Preface

The Author of the present work wishes to state that the Vocabulary, which forms part of it, has existed in manuscript for many years. It is one of several vocabularies of various dialects of the Gypsy tongue, made by him in different countries. The most considerable — that of the dialect of the Zincali or Rumijelies (Romany Chals) of Spain — was published in the year 1841. Amongst those which remain unpublished is one of the Transylvanian Gypsy, made principally at Kolosvār in the year 1844.

"Can you rokra Romany?
Can you play the bosh?
Can you jal adrey the staripen?
Can you chin the cost?"
"Can you speak the Roman tongue?
Can you play the fiddle?
Can you eat the prison-loaf?
Can you cut and whittle?"

Contents

The English Gypsy Language

The Gypsies of England call their language, as the Gypsies of many other countries call theirs, *Romany* or *Romanes*, a word either derived from the Indian *Ram* or *Rama*, which signifies a husband, or from the town Rome, which took its name either from the Indian *Ram*, or from the Gaulic word, *Rom*, which is nearly tantamount to husband or man, for as the Indian *Ram* means a husband or man, so does the Gaulic *Rom* signify that which constitutes a man and enables him to become a husband.

Before entering on the subject of the English Gypsy, I may perhaps be expected to say something about the original Gypsy tongue. It is, however, very difficult to say with certainty anything on the subject. There can be no doubt that a veritable Gypsy tongue at one time existed, but that it at present exists there is great doubt indeed. The probability is that the Gypsy at present exists only in dialects more or less like the language originally spoken by the Gypsy or Zingaro race. Several dialects of the Gypsy are to be found which still preserve along with a considerable number of seemingly original words certain curious grammatical forms, quite distinct from those of any other speech. Others are little more than jargons, in which a certain number of Gypsy words are accommodated to the grammatical forms of the languages of particular countries. In the foremost class of the purer Gypsy dialects, I have no hesitation in placing those of Russia, Wallachia, Bulgaria, and Transylvania. They are so alike, that he who speaks one of them can make himself very well understood by those who speak any of the rest; from whence it may reasonably be inferred that none of them can differ much from the original Gypsy speech; so that when speaking of Gypsy language, any one of these may be taken as a standard.

One of them — I shall not mention which — I have selected for that purpose, more from fancy than any particular reason.

The Gypsy language, then, or what with some qualification I may call such, may consist of some three thousand words, the greater part of which are decidedly of Indian origin, being connected with the Sanscrit or some other Indian dialect; the rest consist of words picked up by the Gypsies from various languages in their wanderings from the East. It has two genders, masculine and feminine; *o* represents the masculine and *i* the feminine: for example, *boro rye*, a great gentleman; *bori rani*, a great lady. There is properly no indefinite article: *gajo* or *gorgio*, a man or gentile; *o gajo*, the man. The noun has two numbers, the singular and the plural. It has various cases formed by postpositions, but has, strictly speaking, no genitive. It has prepositions as well as postpositions; sometimes the preposition is used with the noun and sometimes the postposition: for example, *cad o gav*, from the town; *chungale mannochendar*, evil men from, *i.e.* from evil men. The verb has no infinitive; in lieu thereof, the conjunction 'that' is placed before some person of some tense. 'I wish to go' is expressed in Gypsy by *camov te jaw*, literally, I wish that I go; thou wishest to go, *caumes te jas*, thou wishest that thou goest; *caumen te jallan*, they wish that they go. Necessity is expressed by the impersonal verb and the conjunction 'that': *hom te jav*, I must go; lit. I am that I go; *shan te jallan*, they are that they go; and so on. There are words to denote the numbers from one up to a thousand. For the number nine there are two words, *nu* and *ennyo*. Almost all the Gypsy numbers are decidedly connected with the Sanscrit.

After these observations on what may be called the best preserved kind of Gypsy, I proceed to a lower kind, that of England. The English Gypsy speech is very scanty, amounting probably to not more than fourteen hundred words, the greater part of which seem to be of Indian origin. The rest form a strange medley taken by the Gypsies from various Eastern and Western languages: some few are Arabic, many are Persian; some are Sclavo-Wallachian, others genuine Sclavonian. Here and there a Modern Greek or Hungarian word is discoverable; but in the whole English Gypsy tongue I have never noted but one French word —

namely, *tass* or *dass*, by which some of the very old Gypsies occasionally call a cup.

Their vocabulary being so limited, the Gypsies have of course words of their own only for the most common objects and ideas; as soon as they wish to express something beyond these they must have recourse to English, and even to express some very common objects, ideas, and feelings, they are quite at a loss in their own tongue, and must either employ English words or very vague terms indeed. They have words for the sun and the moon, but they have no word for the stars, and when they wish to name them in Gypsy, they use a word answering to 'lights.' They have a word for a horse and for a mare, but they have no word for a colt, which in some other dialects of the Gypsy is called *kuro*; and to express a colt they make use of the words *tawno gry*, a little horse, which after all may mean a pony. They have words for black, white, and red, but none for the less positive colours — none for grey, green, and yellow. They have no definite word either for hare or rabbit; *shoshoi*, by which they generally designate a rabbit, signifies a hare as well, and *kaun-engro*, a word invented to distinguish a hare, and which signifies ear-fellow, is no more applicable to a hare than a rabbit, as both have long ears. They have no certain word either for to-morrow or yesterday, *collico* signifying both indifferently. A remarkable coincidence must here be mentioned, as it serves to show how closely related are Sanscrit and Gypsy. *Shoshoi* and *collico* are nearly of the same sound as the Sanscrit *sasa* and *kalya*, and exactly of the same import; for as the Gypsy *shoshoi* signifies both hare and rabbit, and *collico* to-morrow as well as yesterday, so does the Sanscrit *sasa* signify both hare and rabbit and *kalya* to-morrow as well as yesterday.

The poverty of their language in nouns the Gypsies endeavour to remedy by the frequent use of the word *engro*. This word affixed to a noun or verb turns it into something figurative, by which they designate, seldom very appropriately, some object for which they have no positive name. *Engro* properly means a fellow, and *engri*, which is the feminine or neuter modification, a thing. When the noun or verb terminates in a vowel, *engro* is turned into *mengro*, and *engri* into *mengri*. I have already shown how, by affixing *engro* to *kaun*, the Gypsies have invented a word to express a

11

hare. In like manner, by affixing *engro* to *pov*, earth, they have coined a word for a potato, which they call *pov-engro* or *pov-engri*, earth-fellow or thing; and by adding *engro* to *rukh*, or *mengro* to *rooko*, they have really a very pretty figurative name for a squirrel, which they call *rukh-engro* or *rooko-mengro*, literally a fellow of the tree. *Poggra-mengri*, a breaking thing, and *pea-mengri*, a drinking thing, by which they express, respectively, a mill and a teapot, will serve as examples of the manner by which they turn verbs into substantives. This method of finding names for objects, for which there are properly no terms in Gypsy, might be carried to a great length — much farther, indeed, than the Gypsies are in the habit of carrying it: a slack-rope dancer might be termed *bittitardranoshellokellimengro*, or slightly-drawn-rope-dancing fellow; a drum, *duicoshtcurenomengri*, or a thing beaten by two sticks; a tambourine, *vangustrecurenimengri*, or a thing beaten by the fingers; and a fife, *muipudenimengri*, or thing blown by the mouth. All these compound words, however, would be more or less indefinite, and far beyond the comprehension of the Gypsies in general.

The verbs are very few, and with two or three exceptions expressive only of that which springs from what is physical and bodily, totally unconnected with the mind, for which, indeed, the English Gypsy has no word; the term used for mind, *zi* — which is a modification of the Hungarian *sziv* — meaning heart. There are such verbs in this dialect as to eat, drink, walk, run, hear, see, live, die; but there are no such verbs as to hope, mean, hinder, prove, forbid, teaze, soothe. There is the verb *apasavello*, I believe; but that word, which is Wallachian, properly means being trusted, and was incorporated in the Gypsy language from the Gypsies obtaining goods on trust from the Wallachians, which they never intended to pay for. There is the verb for love, *camova*; but that word is expressive of physical desire, and is connected with the Sanscrit *Cama*, or Cupid. Here, however, the English must not triumph over the Gypsies, as their own verb 'love' is connected with a Sanscrit word signifying 'lust.' One pure and abstract metaphysical verb the English Gypsy must be allowed to possess — namely, *penchava*, I think, a word of illustrious origin, being derived from the Persian *pendashtan*.

The English Gypsies can count up to six, and have the numerals for ten and twenty, but with those for seven, eight, and nine, perhaps not three Gypsies in England are acquainted. When they wish to express those numerals in their own language, they have recourse to very uncouth and roundabout methods, saying for seven, *dui trins ta yeck*, two threes and one; for eight, *dui stors*, or two fours; and for nine, *desh sore but yeck*, or ten all but one. Yet at one time the English Gypsies possessed all the numerals as their Transylvanian, Wallachian, and Russian brethren still do; even within the last fifty years there were Gypsies who could count up to a hundred. These were *tatchey Romany*, real Gypsies, of the old sacred black race, who never slept in a house, never entered a church, and who, on their death-beds, used to threaten their children with a curse, provided they buried them in a churchyard. The two last of them rest, it is believed, some six feet deep beneath the moss of a wild, hilly heath, — called in Gypsy the *Heviskey Tan*, or place of holes; in English, Mousehold, — near an ancient city, which the Gentiles call Norwich, and the Romans the *Chong Gav*, or the town of the hill.

With respect to Grammar, the English Gypsy is perhaps in a worse condition than with respect to words. Attention is seldom paid to gender; *boro rye* and *boro rawnie* being said, though at *rawnie* is feminine, *bori* and not *boro* should be employed. The proper Gypsy plural terminations are retained in nouns, but in declension prepositions are generally substituted for postpositions, and those prepositions English. The proper way of conjugating verbs is seldom or never observed, and the English method is followed. They say, I *dick*, I see, instead of *dico*; I *dick'd*, I saw, instead of *dikiom*; if I had *dick'd*, instead of *dikiomis*. Some of the peculiar features of Gypsy grammar yet retained by the English Gypsies will be found noted in the Dictionary.

I have dwelt at some length on the deficiencies and shattered condition of the English Gypsy tongue; justice, however, compels me to say that it is far purer and less deficient than several of the continental Gypsy dialects. It preserves far more of original Gypsy peculiarities than the French, Italian, and Spanish dialects, and its words retain more of the original Gypsy form than the words of those

13

three; moreover, however scanty it may be, it is far more copious than the French or the Italian Gypsy, though it must be owned that in respect to copiousness it is inferior to the Spanish Gypsy, which is probably the richest in words of all the Gypsy dialects in the world, having names for very many of the various beasts, birds, and creeping things, for most of the plants and fruits, for all the days of the week, and all the months in the year; whereas most other Gypsy dialects, the English amongst them, have names for only a few common animals and insects, for a few common fruits and natural productions, none for the months, and only a name for a single day — the Sabbath — which name is a modification of the Modern Greek *κυριακὴ*.

Though the English Gypsy is generally spoken with a considerable alloy of English words and English grammatical forms, enough of its proper words and features remain to form genuine Gypsy sentences, which shall be undestood not only by the Gypsies of England, but by those of Russia, Hungary, Wallachia, and even of Turkey; for example: —

> Kek man camov te jib bolli-mengreskoenaes,
> Man camov te jib weshenjugalogonaes.

> I do not wish to live like a baptized person.*
> I wish to live like a dog of the wood.†

It is clear-sounding and melodious, and well adapted to the purposes of poetry. Let him who doubts peruse attentively the following lines: —

> Coin si deya, coin se dado?
> Pukker mande drey Romanes,
> Ta mande pukkeravava tute.

> Rossar-mescri minri deya!
> Wardo-mescro minro dado!
> Coin se dado, coin si deya?
> Mande's pukker'd tute drey Romanes;
> Knau pukker tute mande.

---

* A Christian.   † A fox.

Petulengro minro dado,
Purana minri deya!
Tatchey Romany si men —
Mande's pukker'd tute drey Romanes,
Ta tute's pukker'd mande.

The first three lines of the above ballad are perhaps the oldest specimen of English Gypsy at present extant, and perhaps the purest. They are at least as old as the time of Elizabeth, and can pass among the Zigany in the heart of Russia for Ziganskie. The other lines are not so ancient. The piece is composed in a metre something like that of the ancient Sclavonian songs, and contains the questions which two strange Gypsies, who suddenly meet, put to each other, and the answers which they return.

In using the following Vocabulary the Continental manner of pronouncing certain vowels will have to be observed: thus *ava* must be pronounced like *auva*, according to the English style; *ker* like *kare*, *miro* like *meero*, *zi* like *zee*, and *puro* as if it were written *pooro*.

Romano Lavo-Lil
Word-book of the Romany

A

Abri, *ad. prep.* Out, not within, abroad: soving abri, sleeping abroad, not in a house. *Celtic*, Aber (the mouth or outlet of a river).

Acai ⎫ *ad.* Here.
Acoi ⎭

Adje, *v.n.* To stay, stop. *See* Atch, az.

Adrey, *prep.* Into.

Ajaw, *ad.* So. *Wallachian*, Asha.

Aladge, *a.* Ashamed. *Sans.* Latch, laj.

Aley, *ad.* Down: soving aley, lying down; to kin aley, to buy off, ransom. *Hun.* Ala, alat.

Amande, *pro. pers. dat.* To me.

An, *v. a. imp.* Bring: an lis opré, bring it up.

Ana, *v. a.* Bring. *Sans.* Ani.

Ando, *prep.* In.

Anglo, *prep.* Before.

Apasavello, *v. n.* I believe.

Apopli, *ad.* Again. *Spanish Gypsy*, Apala (after). *Wal.* Apoi (then, afterwards).

Apré, *ad. prep.* Up: kair lis apré, do it up. *Vid.* Opré.

Aranya ⎫ *s.* Lady. *Hungarian Gypsy*, Aranya. *See* Rawnie.
Araunya ⎭

Artav ⎫ *v. a.* To pardon, forgive. *Wal.* Ierta. *Span Gyp.*
Artavello ⎭ Estomar.

Artapen, *s.* Pardon, forgiveness.

Artáros. Arthur.

Asā ⎫ *ad.* Also, likewise, too: meero pal asau, my brother
Asau ⎭ also.

Asarlas, *ad.* At all, in no manner.

Asa. An affix used in forming the second person singular of the present tense; *e.g.* camasa, thou lovest.

Astis, *a.* Possible, it is possible: astis mangué, I can; astis lengué, they can.

Ashā | *ad.* So: ashaw sorlo, so early. *Wal.* Asha. *See* Ajaw.
Ashaw |

Atch, *v.n.* To stay, stop.

Atch opré. Keep up.

Atraish, *a. part.* Afraid. *Sans.* Tras (to fear), atrāsīt (frightened). *See* Traish.

Av, *imperat.* of Ava, to come: av abri, come out.

Ava, *ad.* Yes. *Sans.* Eva.

Ava, *v.a.* To come.

Avata acoi. Come thou here.

Avali, *ad.* Yes. *Wal.* Aieva (really).

Avava. An affix by which the future tense of a verb is formed, *e.g.* mor-avava, I will kill. *See* Vava.

Aukko, *ad.* Here.

Az, *v.n.* To stay.

B

Bal, *s.* Hair. *Tibetian,* Bal (wool). *Sans.* Bala (hair).

Baleneskoe, *a.* Hairy.

Balormengro. A hairy fellow; Hearne, the name of a Gypsy tribe.

Balanser, *s.* The coin called a sovereign.

Ballivas, *s.* Bacon. *Span. Gyp.* Balibá.

Bangalo, *a.* Devilish. *See* Beng, bengako.

Bango, *a.* Left, sinister, wrong, false: bango wast, the left hand; to saulohaul bango, like a plastra-mengro, to swear bodily like a Bow-street runner. *Sans.* Pangu (lame). *Hun.* Pang, pangó (stiff, lazy, paralysed).

Bar, *s.* A stone, a stoneweight, a pound sterling. *Span. Gyp.* Bar. *Hun. Gyp.* Bar. *Hindustani,* Puthur. *Wal.* Piatre. *Fr.* Pierre. *Gr.* βάρος (weight).

Bareskey, *a.* Stony.

Bark, *s.* Breast, woman's breast.

Bas | *s.* Pound sterling. *Wal.* Pes (a weight, burden).
Base |

Bas-engro, *s.* A shepherd. *Hun.* Bacso.

Bashadi, *s.* A fiddle.

Bata, *s.* A bee. *Sans.* Pata.

Bau, *s.* Fellow, comrade. *See* Baw.

Baul, *s.* Snail. *See* Bowle.

Baulo, *s.* Pig, swine. The proper meaning of this word is anything swollen, anything big or bulky. It is connected with the English bowle or bole, the trunk of a tree; also with bowl, boll, and belly; also with whale, the largest of fish, and wale, a tumour; also with the Welsh *bol*, a belly, and *bala*, a place of springs and eruptions. It is worthy of remark that the English word pig, besides denoting the same animal as *baulo*, is of the same original import, being clearly derived from the same root as big, that which is bulky, and the Turkish *buyuk*, great, huge, vast.

Baulie-mas, *s.* Pork, swine's flesh.

Bavano. Windy, broken-winded.

Bavol, *s.* Wind, air. *Sans.* Pavana. *See* Beval.

Bavol-engro, *s.* A wind-fellow; figurative name for a ghost.

Baw, bau, *s.* Fellow, comrade: probably the same as the English country-word baw, bor. *Ger.* Bauer. Av acoi, baw, Come here, fellow. Boer, in wallachian, signifies a boyard or lord.

Beano, *part. pass.* Born.

Beano abri. Born out of doors, like a Gypsy or vagrant.

Bebee, *s.* Aunt. *Rus.* Baba (grandmother, old woman, hag); Baba Yagā, the female demon of the Steppes.

Beng
Bengui } *s.* Devil. *Sans* Pangka (mud). According to the Hindu mythology, there is a hell of mud; the bengues of the Gypsies seem to be its tenants.

Bengako tan, *s.* Hell. Lit. place belonging to devils.

Bengeskoe potan. Devil's tinder, sulphur.

Bengeskoe
Benglo } *a.* Devilish.

Bengree, *s.* Waistcoat. *Span. Gyp.* Blani. *Wal.* (Blāni fur).

Berro, béro, *s.* A ship, a hulk for convicts. *Span. Gyp.* Bero, las galeras, the galleys; presidio, convict garrison.

Ber-engro, *s.* A sailor.

Bero-rukh, *s.* A mast.

Bersh
Besh } *s.* A year. *Sans.* Varsha. He could cour drey his besh, he could fight in his time.

Bershor, *pl.* Years.

19

Besh, *v. n.* To sit: beshel, he sits.

Beshaley |
Beshly   Gypsy name of the Stanley tribe.

Besh-engri, *s.* A chair. *See* Skammen.

Beti, *a.* Little, small.

Beval, *s.* Wind. *See* Bavol.

Bi, *prep.* Without: bi luvvu, without money.

Bicunyie, *a.* Alone, undone: meklis *or* mukalis bicunyie, let it alone.

Bikhin |
Bin   *v. a.* To sell. *Hin.* Bikna.

Bikhnipen, *s.* Sale.

Birk, *s.* Woman's breast. *See* Bark.

Bis, *a.* Twenty.

Bisheni, *s.* The ague.

Bitch |
Bitcha   *v. a.* To send. *Sans.* Bis, bisa.

Bitched |
Bitcheno   *part. pass.* Sent

Bitcheno pawdel. Sent across, transported.

Bitti, *s. a.* Small, piece, a little. This word is not true Gypsy.

Bloen |
Blowing   A cant word, but of Gypsy origin, signifying a sister in debauchery, as Pal denotes a brother in villainy. It is the Plani and Beluñi of the Spanish Gypsies, by whom sometimes Beluñi is made to signify queen; *e.g.* Beluñi de o tarpe (tem opré), the Queen of Heaven, the Virgin. Blowen is used by Lord Byron, in his 'Don Juan.' Speaking of the highwayman whom the Don shoots in the vicinity of London, he says that he used to go to such-and-such places of public resort with — his blowen.

Bob, *s.* A bean. *Wal.* Bob: *pl.* bobbis, bobs.

Boccalo, *a.* Hungry: boccalé pers, hungry bellies.

Bokht, *s.* Luck, fortune: kosko bokht, good luck. *Sans.* Bhāgya. *Pers.* Bakht.

Bokra, *s.* A sheep. *Hun.* Birka.

Bokra-choring. Sheep-stealing.

Bokkar-engro, *s.* A shepherd: bokkar-engro drey, the dude. man in the moon.

Bokkari-gueri, *s.* Shepherdess.

Bokkeriskoe, *a.* Sheepish, belonging to a sheep: bokkeriskey piré, sheep's feet.

Bolla, *v. a.* To baptize.

Bonnek, *s.* Hold: lel bonnek, to take hold.

Booko, *s.* Liver. *See* Bucca.

Bolleskoe divvus. Christmas-day; *query*, baptismal day. *Wal.* Botex (baptism).

Bollimengreskoenaes. After the manner of a Christian.

Boogones, *s.* Smallpox, pimples. *See* Bugnior.

Bor, *s.* A hedge.

Boona, *a.* Good. *Lat.* Bonus. *Wal.* Boun.

Booty, *s.* Work.

Bori, *a. fem.* Big with child, enceinte.

Booty, *v. a.* To work, labour.

Boro, *a.* Great, big. *Hin.* Bura. *Mod. Gr.* βαρὺς (heavy).

Borobeshemeskeguero, *s.* Judge, *great-sitting-fellow*.

Boro Gav. London, big city. *See* Lundra.

Boronashemeskrutan. Epsom race-course.

Bosh, *s.* Fiddle. *Pers.* بازی بار Bazee, baz (play, joke), whence the English cant word 'bosh.' *See* Bashadi.

Boshomengro, *s.* Fiddler.

Bosno ⎰ *s.* A cock, male-bird. *Sans.* Puchchin. *Wal.* Bosh
Boshno ⎱   (testicle). *Gaelic*, Baois (libidinousness).

Boshta, *s.* A saddle.

Bostaris, *s.* A bastard.

Bovalo, *a.* Rich. *Sans.* Bala (strong).

Bowle, *s.* Snail. *See* Baul.

Brishen ⎰ *s.* Rain. *Hun. Gyp.* Breshino. *Sans.* Vrish. *Mod.*
Brisheno ⎱   *Gr.* βρέξιμον.

Brisheneskey, *a.* Rainy: brisheneskey rarde, a rainy night; brisheneskey chiros, a time of rain. *Mod Gr.* καιρὸς βροχερός.

Bucca, *s.* Liver. *Sans.* Bucca (heart). *Wal.* Phikat.

Bucca naflipen, *s.* Liver-complaint.

Buchee, *s.* Work, labour. *See* Butsi.

Buddigur, *s.* A shop. *Span.* Bodega.

Buddikur divvus, *s.* Shopping-day: Wednesday, Saturday.

Bugnes ⎰ *s. pl.* Smallpox, blisters. *Gael.* Boc (a pimple),
Bugnior ⎱   bolg (a blister), bolgach (small-pox). *Wal.*   Mougour (a bud). *Fr.* Bourgeon.

Buklo, *a.* Hungry: buklo tan, hungry spot, a common.

Hun. Gyp. Buklo tan (a wilderness).

Bul, *s.* Rump, buttock.

Bungshoror | *s. pl.* Corks.
Bungyoror |

Busnis | *s. pl.* Spurs, prickles. *Mod. Gr.* βάσανον (pain,
Busnior | torment).

Buroder, *ad.* More: *ad.* ne buroder, no more.

Bute, *a. ad.* Much, very. *Hin.* Būt.

Butsi | *s.* Work, labour.
Buty |

Butying. Working.

C

Caen | *v. n.* To stink.
Cane |

Caenipen | *s.* A stench.
Canipen |

Caeninaflipen, *s.* Stinking sickness, the plague, gaol-fever.
The old cant word Canihen, signifying the gaol-fever, is
derived from this Gypsy term.

Candelo | *a.* Stinking: cannelo mas, stinking meat. *Sans.*
Cannelo | Gandha (smell).

Callico | *s.* To-morrow, also yesterday: collico sorlo, to-
Collico | morrow morning. *Sans.* Kalya. *Hin.* Kal (to-
| morrow, yesterday).

Cana, *ad.* Now: cana sig, now soon. *See* Kanau, knau.

Cam, *s.* The sun. *Hin.* Khan. *Heb.* Khama (the sun), kham
(heat).

Cam. To wish, desire love.

Cam | *v. a.* To love. *Sans.* Cama (love). Cupid; from
Camello | which Sanscrit word the Latin Amor is
Camo | derived.

Cambori | *a.* Pregnant, big with child.
Cambri |

Camlo | Lovel, name of a Gypsy tribe. Lit. amiable. With
Caumlo | this word the English "comely" is connected.

Camo-mescro, *s.* A lover; likewise the name Lovel.

Can, *s.* The sun.

Can, *s.* An ear. *See* Kaun.

Cana, *ad.* Now: cana sig, now soon. *See* Kanau.

Canáfi ⎫
Canapli ⎰ *s.* Turnip

Canairis. A Gypsy name.

Canior ⎫
Caunor ⎰ *s. pl.* Pease.

Canni. A hen. *Span. Gyp.* Cañi. *Hun. Gyp.* Cackni. *Gael.* Cearc.

Cannis. Hens.

Cappi, *s.* Booty, gain, fortune: to lel cappi, to acquire booty, make a capital; a fortune.

Cas, *s.* Hay: cas-stiggur, haystack; cas kairing, hay-making.

Cas, *s.* Cheese. *Lat.* Caseus. This word is used by the pikers or tramps, as well as by the Gypsies. *See* Kael.

Catches ⎫ *s. pl.* Scissors. *Hun.* Kasza. *Wal.* Kositsie (sickle).
Catsau ⎰ *Mod. Gr.* κόσα. *Rus.* Kosa.

Cato, *prep.* To; more properly From. *Hun. Gyp.* Cado. *Wal.* Katre (towards).

Cavo, *pron. dem.* This.

Cavocoi. This here.

Cavocoiskoenœs. In this manner.

Caur, *v. a.* To filch, steal in an artful manner by bending down. *Heb.* כָּרַע Cara, incurvavit se. *Eng.* Cower.

Cayes, *s.* Silk. *Pers.* قَزّ *Span. Gyp.* Quequesa. *Sans.* Kauseya.

Chal, *s.* Lad, boy, son, fellow. Connected with this word is the Scottish Chiel, the Old English Childe, and the Russian Chelovik. *See* Romani chal.

Chăro, *s.* Plate, dish.

Chavali, *s. f.* Girl, damsel.

Chavi, *s. f.* Child, girl, daughter.

Cham, *s.* Leather: chameskie roķunies, leather breeches. *Sans* Charma (skin).

Chavo, *s. m.* Child, son: *pl.* chaves. Cheaus is an old French hunting term for the young ones of a fox.

Charos ⎫
Cheros ⎰ *s.* Heaven. *Wal.* Cher.

Chauvo, *s. See* Chavo.

Chaw, *s.* Grass.

Chawhoktamengro, *s.* Grasshopper, *See* Hokta.

Chee, *a.* No. none: chee butsi, no work. *See* Chi, chichi.

Chericlo, *s.* Bird. *See* Chiriclo.

Chiricleskey tan, *s.* Aviary, birdcage.

Chi, *s. f.* Child, daughter, girl: Romany chi, Gypsy girl.

Chi
Chichi } *s.* Nothing.
Chiti

Chin, *v. a.* To cut: chin lis tuley, cut it down. *Sans.* Chun (to cut off). *Hin.* Chink. *Gaelic*, Sgian (a knife).

Chin the cost. To cut the stick; to cut skewers for butchers and pegs for linen-lines, a grand employment of the Gypsy fellows in the neighbourhood of London.

China-mengri, *s. f.* A letter; a thing incised, marked, written in.

China-mengro, *s.* Hatchet. Lit. cutting-thing.

Chinipen. *s.* A cut.

Ching
Chingaro } *v. a.* To fight, quarrel.

Chinga-guero, *s.* A warrior.

Chingaripen, *s.* War, strife. *Sans.* Sangara.

Chingring, *part. pres.* Fighting, quarrelling.

Chik, *s.* Earth, dirt. *Span. Gyp.* Chique. *Hin.* Chikkar.

Chiklo, a. Dirty.

Chiriclo, *s. m.* Bird. *Hin.* Chiriya.

Chiricli, *s. f.* Hen-bird.

Chiros, *s.* Time. *Mod. Gr.* καιρὸς.

Chiv
Chiva } *v. a.* To cast, fling, throw, place, put: chiv lis
Chuva } tuley, fling it down; chiv oprey, put up. *Rus.*
Kyio (to forge, cast iron). *Sans.* Kship.

Chiving tulipen prey the chokkars. Greasing the shoes.

Chofa, *s. f.* Petticoat.

Chohawni, *s.* Witch. *See* Chovahano.

Chohawno, *s.* Wizard.

Chok, *s.* Watch, watching.

Chok-engro, *s.* Watchman.

Chok, *s.* Shoe: chokkor, chokkors, shoes. *Hun* Czókó (wooden shoe).

Choko-mengro. Shoemaker.

Choka, *s.* Coat.

Chokni
Chukni } *s.* Whip. *Wal.* Chokini (a strap, leather). *Hun.* Csakany (a mace, sledge hammer). *Hun. Gyp.* Chokano (a staff). *Wal.* Chokan, chokinel (a hammer).

Chukni wast, s. The whip-hand, the mastery.

Chollo, a. s. Whole.

Chomany, s. Something. *Span. Gyp.* Cormuñi (some); chimoni (anything). *Wal.* Chineba (some one). For every chomany there's a lav in Romany: there's a name in Gypsy for everything.

Chong, s. Knee. *Hun.* Czomb. *Sans.* Chanu. *Lat.* Genu

Chongor, *pl.* Knees.

Choom ⎫   *v. a.* To kiss. *Sans.* Chumb. Choomande, kiss
Choomava ⎭   me. *Span. Gyp.* Chupendi (a kiss), a corruption of Choomande.

Choomia, s. A kiss.

Choomo-mengro, one of the tribe Boswell.

Choon, s. Moon. *Hun. Gyp.* Chemut. *Sans.* Chandra.

Choot, s. Vinegar. *See* Chute.

Chore, v. a. To steal. *Sans.* Chur.

Chore, s. Thief. *Hin.* Chor

Chories, *pl.* Thieves.

Chor-dudee-mengri, s. Κλεφτοφάναρον (thieves' lantern, dark lantern).

Choredo, a. Poor, poverty stricken. *Sans.* Dāridra.

Choredi, *fem.* of Choredo.

Choriness, s. Poverty.

Choro, a. Poor. *Span. Gyp.* Chororo. *Hin.* Shor.

Chovahan, v. a. To bewitch.

Chovahani ⎫
Chowián   ⎬   s. f. Witch.

Chovahano, s. Wizard.

Choveno, a. Poor, needy, starved. Perhaps derived from the Russian Tchernoe (back, dirty, wretched); or from the Hungarian Csunya (hateful, frightful); whence the Chungalo of the Hungarian, and also of the Spanish Gypsies.

Choveni, *fem.* of Choveno.

Choveno ker, s. Workhouse, poorhouse.

Chukkal, s. Dog. *Span. Gyp.* Chuquel. *Sans.* Kukkura. *Basque*, Chacurra. *See* Juggal.

Chumba, s. Bank, hill. *Russ.* Xolm (a hill).

Chungarava ⎫ *v. a.* To spit. *Wal.* Ckouina. *Hun. Gyp.*
Chungra   ⎭   Chudel (he spits).

Churi, s. Knife. *Sans.* Chhuri. *Hin.* Churi.

Churi-mengro, *s.* Knife-grinder, cutler.

Churo-mengro, *s.* A soldier, swordsman.

Chute, *s.* Vinegar. *Mod Gr.* ζύδι. *Wal.* Otset.

Chute-pavi, *s.* Cyder; perhaps a crap-apple. Lit. vinegar-apple.

Chuvvenhan, *s.* Witch. *See* Chovahani.

Cinerella. Female Gypsy name.

Cocal, *s.* Bone. *Mod. Gr.* κοκκαλον.

Cocalor, *pl.* Bones.

Coco
Cocodus } *s.* Uncle. *Hin.* Caucau.

Cocoro
Cocoros } *a. pro.* Alone, self: tu cocoro, thyself.

Coin, *pro. interrog.* Who? *Hin.* Kaun.

Collor, *s. pl.* Shillings: dui collor a crookos, two shillings a week. In Spanish Germania or cant, two ochavos, or farthings, are called: dui *calés*.

Commorrus, *s.* A room, hall. *Hun.* Kamara. *Hin.* Cumra. *Ger.* Kammer.

Cong, congl, *v. a.* To comb.

Congli
Congro } *s. f.* A comb. *Sans.* Kanagata.

Congri, *s. f.* A church.

Coor
Coorava } *v. a.* To fight. *Irish*, Comhrac [courac]. *Welsh*, Curaw (to beat).

Coorapen, *s.* Fight, a beating: I shall lel a curapen, I shall get a beating.

Cooroboshno, *s.* A fighting cock.

Cooromengro, *s.* Fighter, boxer, soldier.

Coppur, *s.* Blanket. *Rus.* Kovér (a carpet). *Wal.* Kovor, *id.*

Corauni
Corooni } *s.* A crown: medrauliskie corauni, royal crown. *Wal.* Coroan.

Cori, *s.* Thorn. Membrum virile. *Span.* Carajo [caraco]. *Gascon*, Quirogau.

Coro
Coru } *s.* Pot, pitcher, cup: coru levinor, cup of ale; boro coro, a quart. *Span. Gyp.* Coro. *Hin.* Gharā.

Coro-mengro, *s.* Potter.

Coro-mengreskey tem. Staffordshire.

Corredo, *a.* Blind. *Span. Gyp.* Corroro. *Pers.* کور *Wal.* Kior (one-eyed).

Cosht
Cost | s. Stick. *Sans*. Kāshtha.

Cost-engres, *s. pl.* Branch-fellows, people of the New Forest, Stanleys.

Coshtno, *a.* Wooden.

Covar
Covo | s. Thing: covars, things; covar-bikhning-vardo, caravan in which goods are carried about for sale.

Crafni, *s.* Button. *Ger*. Knopf.

Crafni-mengro, *s.* Buttonmaker.

Creeor, *s. pl.* Ants, pismires. *Span. Gyp*. Ocrianse (the ant), quiria (ant).

Cricni
Crookey
Crookauros | s. Week. *See* Curco.
Crookos

Cuesni, *s.* Basket. *See* Cushnee.

Culvato (Gypsy name). Claude.

Curaken, *s.* Fighting. *See* Coorapen.

Curepen, *s.* Trouble, affliction: curepenis, afflictions.

Curkey
Curko | s. Week, Sunday. *Mod. Gr.* κυριακή.

Curlo, *s.* Throat. *Pers.* ﮔﻠﻮ Chin his curlo, cut his throat.

Curlo-mengri, *s.* A ruff, likewise a pillow; anything belonging to the throat or neck.

Cushnee
Cushni | s. Basket. *Wal*. Koshnitse.
Cusnee

Cuttor, *s.* A piece, a guinea-piece: dui cuttor, two guineas; will you lel a cuttor, will you take a bit? sore in cuttors, all in rags.

D

Dad, *s.* Father. *Welsh*, Tâd. *Wal*. Tat. *Rus. Gyp*. Dad.

Dado, *s.* Father. *Rus. Gyp*. Dado.

Dand, *s.* Tooth. *Sans*. Danta.

Danior, *pl.* Teeth.

Dand, *v. a.* To bite.

Daya
Dieya | s. Mother, properly nurse. *Sans*. Dhayas (fostering). *Pers.* ﺩﺍﻳﻪ Daya. *Mod. Gr.* θεὶα. *Rus. Gyp*. Daia. *Wal*. Doika.

27

Deav, *v. a.* Give. *Sans*. Dā. *Wal*. Da.

Del. He gives.

Del-engro, *s.* A kicking-horse.

Del-oprey, *v. a.* To read.

Denne, *ad.* Than.

Der. An *affix*, by which the *comparative* is formed; *e.g.* Wafodu, bad: wafodúder than dovor, worse than they.

Desch, *a.* Ten. *Sans*. Dasan. *Wal*. Zetche.

Desh ta yeck. Eleven.

Desh ta dui. Twelve.

Desh ta trin. Thirteen.

Desh ta store. Fourteen.

Desh ta pansch. Fifteen.

Desh ta sho. Sixteen.

Desh ta eft. Seventeen.

Deschko. Eighteen (?): deshko hori, eighteenpence; properly, Desh ta octo hori.

Devel, *s.* God. *Sans*. Deva. *Lith*. Dēwas. *Lat*. Deus. *See* Dibble, Dovvel, Dubbel.

Develeskoe, *s.* Holy, divine. *Sans*. Deva.

Deyed, *pret. of* Deav. He gave.

Dibble, *s.* God. *See* Devel.

Dic ⎱ *v. n.* To look: dic tuley, look down; dicking misto,
Dico ⎰ looking well. *Sans*. Iksh (to see, look). *Gaelic,* Dearcam (to see); dearc (eye).

Dickimengro, *s.* Overlooker, overseer.

Dicking hev, *s.* A window, seeing-hole.

Die, *s.* Mother. *Rus. Gyp*. Die. *See* Daya.

Dikkipen, *s.* Look, image. *Sans* Driksha (aspect). *Welsh*, Drych (aspect).

Diklo, *s.* Cloth, sheet, shift.

Dinnelo, *s.* A fool, one possessed by the devil. *Wal*. Diniele (of the devil); louat diniele (possessed by the devil).

Dinneleskoe, *a.* Foolish.

Dinneleskoenœs. Like a fool.

dinnelipénes, *s. pl.* Follies, nonsense.

Diverous. A Gypsy name.

Diviou, *a.* Mad: jawing diviou, going mad. *Sans*. Déva (a god, a fool).

Diviou-ker, *s.* Madhouse.

Diviou kokkodus Artáros. Mad Uncle Arthur.

Divvus, *s.* Day. *Sans*. Divasa.

Divveskoe | *a.* Daily: divvuskoe morro, daily bread.
Divvuskoe |

Diximengro, *s.* Overseer. *See* Dickimengro.

Dook, *v. a.* To hurt, bewitch: dook the gry, bewitch the horse. *Wal.* Deokira (to fascinate, bewitch). *See* Duke, dukker.

Dooriya | *s.* Sea. *Pers.* دريا *Irish*, Deire (the deep). *Welsh*,
Dooya | Dwr (water). *Old Irish*, Dobhar.

Dooriva durril, *s.* Currant, plum. *Lit.* Sea-berry.

Dooriya durrileskie guyi, *s.* Plum pudding.

Dori, *s.* Thread, lace: kaulo dori, black lace. *Hin.* Dora.

Dosch | *s.* Evil, harm: kek dosh, no harm. *Sans.* Dush
Dosh | (bad).

Dosta, *s.* Enough. *Wal.* Destoul. *Rus.* Dostaet (it is sufficient). *See* Dusta.

Dou, *imp.* Give: dou mande, give me. *See* Deav.

Dou dass. Cup and saucer. *See* Dui das.

Dovo, *pro. dem.* That: dovó si, that's it.

Dovor. Those, they: wafodúder than dovor, worse than they.

Dov-odoy | *ad.* Yonder.
Dovoy-oduvva |

Dov-odoyskoenaes. In that manner.

Doovel, *s.* God. *See.* Duvvel.

Drab | *s.* Medicine, poison. *Pers.* دارو Daru. *Wal.* Otrav.
Drav |

Drab-engro | *s.* Apothecary, poison-monger.
Drav-engro |

Drab, *v. a.* To poison. *Wal.* Otribi.

Drey, *prep.* In.

Dubble, *s.* God: my dearie Dubbleskey, for my dear God's sake.

Dude, *s.* The moon.

Dudee, *s.* A light, a star. *Sans.* Dyuti.

Dude-bar, *s.* Diamond, light-stone.

Drom, *s.* Road. *Wal.* Drom. *Mod. Gr.* δρόμος.

Drom-luring, *s.* Highway robbery.

Dui, *a.* Two.

Duito, *s.* Second.

Duito divvus, *s.* Tuesday. *Lit.* Second day.

Duidas ⎫
Duitas ⎭ *s.* Cup and saucer.

Duke, *v. a.* To hurt, bewitch. *Sans.* Duhkha (pain). *Heb.* Dui (languor, deadly faintness).

Dukker, *v. a.* To bewitch, tell fortunes. *Wal.* Deokiea (to fascinate, enchant).

Dukker drey my vast. Tell my fortune by my hand.

Dukkering, *s.* Fortune-telling. *Wal.* Deokiere (fasination). *Mod. Gr.* τύχη (fortune).

Dukkipen, *s.* Fortune-telling.

Dukker, *v. n.* To ache: my sherro dukkers, my head aches. *See* Duke, dukker.

Dum ⎫
Dumo ⎭ *s.* Black. *Pers.* دُم (tail).

Dur, *ad.* Far. *Sans.* Dur. *Pers.* دُور

Dur-dicki mengri, *s.* Telescope. Lit. far-seeing thing.

Durro, *ad.* Far.

Durro-der, *ad.* Farther.

Durriken, *s.* Fortune-telling.

Durril, *s.* Any kind of berry, a gooseberry in particular.

Durrilau ⎫
Durilyor ⎭ *pl.* Berries.

Durrileskie guyi, *s.* Gooseberry pudding.

Dusta, *a. s.* Enough, plenty: dusta foky, plenty of people. *See* Dosta.

Duvvel, *s.* God.

E

Eange, *s.* Itch.

Ebyok, *s.* The sea. *Sans.* Aapa (water). *Wal.* Ape.

Eft, *a.* Seven. Few of the English Gypsies are acquainted with this word; consequently, the generality, when they wish to express the number seven, without being understood by the Gorgios or Gentiles, say Dui trins ta yeck, two threes and one.

En. A kind of *genitive particle* used in compound words, being placed between a noun and the particle 'gro' or 'guero,' which signifies a possessor, or that which governs a thing or has to do with it: *e.g.* lav-en-gro, a linguist, or a man of words, lit. word-of-fellow; wesh-engro, a forester, or one who governs the wood; gurush-en-gre, things costing a groat, lit. groat-of-things.

Engri. A *neuter affix*, composed of the particles 'en' and 'gro,' much used in the formation of figurative terms for things of which there are no positive names in English Gypsy: for example, yag-engri, a fire-thing, which denotes a gun; poggra-mengri, a breaking-thing or mill; 'engri' is changed into 'mengri' when the preceding word terminates in a vowel.

Engro. A *masculine affix*, used in the formation of figurative names; for example, kaun-engro, an ear-fellow, or creature with ears, serving to denote a hare; rok-engro, or ruko-mengro, a tree-fellow, denoting a squirrel; it is also occasionally used in names for inanimate objects, as pov-engro, an earth-thing or potato. *See* Guero.

Escunyo, *s.* A wooden skewer, a pin. *Span. Gyp.* Chinga-bar (a pin).

Escunyes, *pl.* Skewers.

Escunye-mengro, *s.* A maker of skewers.

Eskoe, *fem.* Eskie. A particle which affixed to a noun turns it into an adjective: *e.g.* Duvel, God; duveleskoe, divine. It seems to be derived from the *Wal.* Esk, Easkie.

Eskey. An *affix* or *postposition*, signifying, for the sake of: *e.g.* Mi-dubble-eskey, for God's sake.

Ever-komi, *ad.* Evermore.

F

Fake, *v. a.* To work, in a dishonest sense; to steal, pick pockets.

Fakement, *s.* A robbery, any kind of work: a pretty fakement that, a pretty piece of work. A scoundrel — you ratfelo fakement, you precious scoundrel; a man of any kind — he's no bad fakement after all; a girl, St. Paul's Cathedral — what a rinkeny fakement, what a pretty girl, what a noble church.

Fashono, *a.* False, fashioned, made up. *Wal.* Fatche (to make); fatze (face, surface).

Fashono wangustis. Pretended gold rings, made in reality of brass or copper.

Fashono wangust engre. Makers of false rings.

Fenella. A female Gypsy name.

Ferreder, *a*. Better, more. *Gaelic*, Feairde.

Fetér, *ad*. Better. *Pers*. فَتَر *Span*. *Gyp*. Fetér.

Figis, *s*. Fig.

Figis-rookh, *s*. Fig-tree.

Filisen, *s*. Country-seat.

Fino, *a*. Fine. This word is not pure Gypsy: fino covar, a fine thing.

Floure, *s*. Flower; a female Gypsy name.

Fordel, *v. a*. Forgive; generally used for Artav, or Artavello, *q. v*., and composed of the English 'for' and the Gypsy 'del.'

Fordias ⎫
Fordios ⎭ *part. pass*. Forgiven.

Foros, *s*. City. *See* Vauros.

Ful, *s*. Dung: ful-vardo, muck cart.

Fuzyanri, *s*. Fern. *Hun*. Füz (willow), fácska (a shrub), füszár (a stem).

G

Gad, *s*. A shirt: pauno gad, a clean shirt.

Gare, *v. n., v. a*. To take care, beware; to hide, conceal. *Sans*. Ghar, to cover.

Garridan. You hid: luvvu sor garridan, the money which you hid.

Garrivava, *v. a*. I hide or shall hide, take care: to gare his nangipen, to hide his nakedness.

Gav, *s*. A town, village. *Pers*. گُوي

Gav-engro, *s*. A constable, village officer, beadle, citizen.

Gillie, *s*. A song. *Sans*. Khēlī.

Gillies. Songs. Sometimes used to denote newspapers; because these last serve, as songs did in the old time, to give the world information of remarkable events, such as battles, murders, and robberies.

Gilyava. I sing, or shall sing. *Hin*. Guywuya. *Mod. Gr*. κοιλαδῶ.

Gin, *v. a*. To count reckon. *Sans*. Gan. *Hin*. Ginna.

Ginnipen, *s*. A reckoning.

Giv, *s*. Wheat. *Sans*. Yava (barley). *See* Jobis.

Giv-engro, *s.* Wheat-fellow, figurative name for farmer.

Giv-engro ker, *s.* Farmhouse.

Giv-engro puv, *s.* Farm.

Godli, *s.* A warrant, perhaps hue and cry. *See* Gudlie. *Span. Gyp.* Gola (order).

Gono, *s.* A sack. *Hin.* Gon.

Gorgio, *s.* A Gentile, a person who is not a Gypsy; one who lives in a house and not in a tent. It is a modification of the Persian word کوجیا Cojia, which signifies a gentleman, a doctor, a merchant, etc. *Span. Gyp.* Gacho.

Gorgiken rat. Of Gentile blood.

Gorgie, *s.* A female Gentile or Englishwoman.

Gorgikonaes, *ad.* After the manner of Gentiles.

Gooee, *s.* Pudding. *See* Guyi.

Gran, *s.* A barn: I sov'd yeck rarde drey a gran, I slept one night within a barn (Gypsy song).

Gran-wuddur, *s.* A barn door.

Gran-wuddur-chiriclo. Barn-door fowl.

Grasni
Grasnakkur } *s.* Mare, outrageous woman: what a grasni shan tu, what a mare you are! Grasnakkur is sometimes applied to the *mayor* of a town.

Grestur
Gristur } *s.* A horse. *Span. Gyp.* Gras, graste.

Gry, *s.* A horse. *Sans.* Kharu. *Hin.* Ghora. *Irish* and *Scottish Gaelic*, Greadh.

Gry-choring, *s.* Horse-stealing.

Gry-engro, *s.* Horse-dealer.

Gry-nashing. Horse-racing.

Gudlee
Godli } *s.* Cry, noise, shout. *Hin.* Ghooloo. *Irish*, Gúl. *Rus.* Gyl = gool (shout); Gólos (voice).

Grommena
Grovena
Grubbena } *s.* and *v.* Thunder, to thunder. *Sans.* Garjana. *Rus.* Grom (thunder). *Heb.* Ream, raemah. *Gaelic*, Gairm (a cry).

Gudlo, *a., s.* Sweet; honey, sugar.

Gudlo-pishen, *s.* Honey-insect, bee. *See* Bata.

Gué. An *affix*, by which the dative case is formed: *e.g.* Man, I; mangué, to me.

Guero, *s.* A person, fellow, that which governs, operates. *Sans.* Kāra (a maker). *Pers.* ک *Welsh*, Gwr (a man). In the Spanish cant language, Guro signifies an alguazil, a kind of civil officer. *See* Engro.

Gueri, *s. f.* Female person, virgin: Mideveleskey gueri Mary, Holy Virgin Mary.

Gush
Gurush ⎱ *a.* Groat: gurushengri, a groat's worth.
Gurushi ⎰

Guveni, *s.* Cow. *Sans.* Go.

Guveni-bugnior, *s.* Cow-pox.

Guveno, *s.* A bull. *Sans.* Gavaya. *Gaelic*, Gavuin, gowain (year-old-calf).

Guyi, *s.* Pudding, black pudding. *Hin.* Gulgul. *Span. Gyp.* Golli.

Guyi-mengreskie tan, *s.* Yorkshire. Lit. pudding-eaters country; in allusion to the puddings for which Yorkshire is celebrated.

H

Ha ⎱ *v. a.* To eat.
Haw ⎰

Habben, *s.* Food, victuals.

Hal, *v. a.* To eat: mande can't hal lis, I can't eat it. *Sans.* Gala.

Hanlo, *s.* A landlord, innkeeper. *Span. Gyp.* Anglanó.

Hatch, *v. a.* To burn, light a fire.

Hatchipen, *s.* A burning.

Hatch, *v. n.* To stay, stop. *See* Adje, atch, az.

Hatchi-witchu, *s.* A hedgehog. This is a compound word from the *Wal.* Aritche, a hedgehog, and the Persian Besha, a wood, and signifies properly the prickly thing of the wood. In Spanish Gypsy, one of the words for a pig or hog is Eriche, evidently the Wallachian Aritche, a hedgehog.

Hekta, *s.* Haste: kair hekta, make haste; likewise a leap. *See* Hokta. *Sans.* Hat'ha (to leap).

Heres ⎱ *s. pl.* Legs. *Span. Gyp.* Jerias. Coshtni herri (a
Heris ⎰ wooden leg).

Hetavava, *v. a.* To slay, beat, hit, carry off, plunder: if I can lel bonnek of tute hetavava tute, if I can lay hold of you I will slay you. *Heb.* Khataf (rapuit). *Sans.* Hat'ha (to ill-use, rapere).

Hev, *s.* Hole: pawnugo hev, a water hole, a well; hev, a window; hevior, windows. *Sans.* Avata.

Heviskey, *a.* Full of holes: heviskey tan, a place full of holes.

Hin, *s.* Dirt, ordure. *Mod. Gr.*χυτὸν. *Wal.* Gounoiou. *Irish*, Gaineamh (sand).

Hin, *v. a.* To avoid ordure. *Sans.* Hanna. *Mod. Gr.* χύνω.

Hindity-mengré ⎫
Hindity-mescré ⎬ *s. pl. Irish.* Dirty, sordid fellows.

Hoffeno, *s.* A liar.

Hok-hornie-mush, *s.* A policeman. Partly a cant word.

Hokka, *v. n.* To lie, tell a falsehood: hokka tute mande, if you tell me a falsehood.

Hokkano, *s.* A lie. *Sans.* Kuhanā (hypocrisy).

Hokta, *v. a.* To leap, jump. *See* Hekta.

Hokta-mengro, *s.* Leaper, jumper.

Hoofa, *s.* A cap.

Hor ⎫
Horo ⎬ *s.* A penny. *Span. Gyp.* Corio an ochavo (or farthing).

Horry, *s. pl.* Pence: shohorry, showhawry, sixpence.

Horsworth, *s.* Pennyworth.

Horkipen, *s.* Copper. *Hun. Gyp.* Harko.

Huffeno, *s.* A liar. *See* Hoffeno.

Hukni, *s.* Ringing the changes, the fraudulent changing of one thing for another.

I

I, *pro.* She, it.

I., A *feminine* and *neuter termination*: e.g. Yag engri, a fire-thing or gun; coin si, who is she? so si, what is it?

Inna ⎫ *prep.* In, within: inner Lundra, in London. *Span.*
Inner ⎬ *Gyp.* Enré.

Iouzia, *s.* A flower.

Is, *conj.* If; it is affixed to the verb — *e.g.* Dikiomis, if I had seen.

Iv, *s.* Snow. *Hun. Gyp.* Yiv. *Span. Gyp.* Give.

Iv-engri ⎫
Ivi-mengri ⎬ *s.* Snow-thing, snowball.

Iuziou, *a.* Clean. *Mod. Gr.* ὑγιὴς (sound, healthy). *See* Roujio.

J

Jal.　To go, walk, journey. This verb is allied to various words in different languages signifying movement, course or journey: — to the Sanscrit Il, ila, to go; to the Russian Gulliat, to stroll, to walk about; to the Turkish Iel, a journey; to the Jol of the Norse, and the Yule of the Anglo-Saxons, terms applied to Christmas-tide, but which properly mean the circular journey which the sun has completed at that season: for what are Jol and Yule but the Ygul of the Hebrews? who call the zodiac 'Ygul ha mazaluth,' or the circle of the signs. It is, moreover, related to the German Jahr and the English Year, radically the same words as Jol, Yule, and Ygul, and of the same meaning — namely, the circle travelled by the sun through the signs.

Já, *v. imp.*　Go thou!

Jal amande.　I shall go.

Jal te booty.　Go to work.

Jalno ⎫
Java ⎬ *v. a.*　I go. *Sans.* Chara.
Jaw ⎭

Jas, jasa.　Thou goest: tute is jasing, thou art going.

Jal, *3rd pers. pres.*　He goes.

Jalla, *f.*　She goes.

Jalno ando pawni, *v. a.*　I swim. Lit. I go in water.

Jaw, *ad.*　So: jaw si, so it is. *See* Ajaw, asá, ashá.

Jib, *s.*　Tongue. *Sans.* Jihva.

Jib, *v. n.*　To live, to exist. *Sans.* Jiv. *Rus.* Jit. *Lithuanian*, Gywenu.

Jibben, *s.*　Life, livelihood. *Sans.* Jīvata (life), Jīvika (livelihood). *Rus.* Jivot, Tchivot.

Jivvel, *v. n.*　He lives: kai jivvel o, where does he live?

Jin ⎫
Jinava ⎬ *v. n.*　To know. *Sans.* Jna.

Jinnepen, *s.*　Wisdom, knowledge. *Sans.* Jnapti (understanding).

Jinney-mengro, *s.*　A knowing fellow, a deep card, a Grecian, a wise man, a philosopher.

Jinney-mengreskey rokrapénes.　Sayings of the wise: the tatcho drom to be a jinney-mengro is to dick and rig in zi, the true way to be a wise man is to see and bear in mind.

Jongar, *v. n.* To awake. *Sans.* Jagri. *Hin.* Jugana.

Jôbis, *s.* Oats. *Sans.* Java (barley). *Wal.* Obiz. *See* Giv.

Joddakaye, *s.* Apron; anything tied round the middle or hips. *Sans.* Kata (the hip, the loins), Kataka (a girdle).

Ju, *s.* A louse. *Sans.* Yuka.

Juvalo, *a.* Lousy.

Juvior, *s. pl.* Lice.

Juggal ⎫
Jukkal ⎭ *s.* Dog. *Sans.* Srigāla (jackal).

Jukkalor. Dogs.

Jukkaelsti cosht, *s.* Dog-wood; a hard wood used for making skewers.

Juva ⎫
Juvali ⎭ Woman, wife.

Juvli, *s.* Girl. *See* Chavali.

K

Kael, *s.* Cheese.

Kaes, *s.* Cheese.

Kah ⎫ *ad.* Where: kai tiro ker, where's your house? kai si
Kai ⎭ the churi, where is the knife? *Sans.* Kva.

Kair, *v. a.* To do. *Sans.* Kri, to do; kara (doing).

Kair misto. To make well, cure, comfort.

Kairipen, *s.* Work, labour. *Sans.* Karman.

Kakkaratchi, *s.* Magpie; properly a raven. *Mod. Gr.* κορακαζ.

Kanau ⎫
Knau ⎭ *ad.* Now.

Karring. Crying out, hawking goods. *Span. Gyp.* Acarar (to call). *See* Koring.

Kaulo, *a.* Black. *Sans* Kāla. *Arab.* كالو

Kaulo chiriclo, *s.* A blackbird.

Kaulo cori, *s.* A blackthorn.

Kaulo durril, *s.* Blackberry.

Kaulo Gav, *s.* Black-town, Birmingham.

Kaulo guero, *s.* A black, negro.

Kaulo guereskey tem, *s.* Negroland, Africa.

Kaulo-mengro, *s.* A blacksmith.

Kaulo ratti. Black blood, Gypsy blood: kaulo ratti adrey leste, he has Gypsy blood in his veins.

Kaun, *s.* An ear. *Sans.* Karna.

Kaun-engro, *s.* An ear-fellow, thing with long ears; a figurative name for a hare.

Ke, *prep.* Unto. Likewise a *postposition* — *e.g.* lenké, to them.

Keir ⎫
Ker ⎭ *s.* A house. *Sans.* Griha.

Kerey ⎫
Keri ⎭ *ad.* Home, homeward: java keri, I will go home.

Keir-poggring. House-breaking.

Keir-rakli, *s.* A housemaid.

Kek, *ad. a.* No, none, not: kek tatcho, it is not true.

Kekkeno, *a.* None, not any: kekkeni pawni, no water.

Kekkeno mushe's poov, *s.* No man's land; a common.

Kekkauvi, *s. f.* Kettle. *Mod. Gr.* κακκάβη.

Kekkauviskey saster, *s.* Kettle-iron; the hook by which the kettle is suspended over the fire.

Kekko, *ad.* No, it is not, not it, not he.

Kekkomi. No more. *See* Komi, Ever-komi.

Kek-cushti. Of no use; no good. *See* Koshto.

Kem, *s.* The sun. *See* Cam.

Ken. A *particle* affixed in English Gypsy to the name of a place terminating in a vowel, in order to form a genitive; *e.g.* Eli*ken* bori congri, the great church of Ely. *See* En.

Ken, *s.* A house, properly a nest. *Heb.* קן Kin.

Kenyor, *s. pl.* Ears. *See* Kaun.

Ker ⎫
Kerava ⎭ *v. a.* To do; make: kair yag, make a fire. *Sans.* Kri. *Pers.* کردن *Gaelic*, Ceaird (a trade), ceard (a tinker). *Lat.* Cerdo (a smith). *English*, Char, chare (to work by the day).

Kerdo. He did.

Kedast, *2nd pers. pret.* Thou didst.

Kedo, *part. pass.* Done.

Kerri-mengro, *s.* Workman.

Kerrimus, *s.* Doing, deed: mi-Doovel's kerrimus, the Lord's doing. *Sans.* Karman (work).

Kerrit, *p. pass.* Cooked, boiled. Anglo-Indian word, Curried. *Fr.* Cuire. *Gaelic*, Greidh (to cook victuals).

Kettaney, *ad.* Together. *Wal.* Ketziba (many). *See* Kisi.

Kidda, *v. a.* To pluck.

Kil, *v. a.* To dance, play. *Hin.* Kelná. *Sans.* Kshvel.

Killi-mengro, *s.* A dancer, player.

Kil, *s.* Butter.

Kin, *v. a.* To buy: kinning and bikkning, buying and selling. *Heb.* Kana (he bought).

Kin aley. To ransom, redeem, buy off.

Kinnipen, *s.* A purchase.

Kinnipen-divvus, *s.* Purchasing-day, Saturday.

Kindo, a. Wet.

Kipsi, *s.* Basket. *Span. Gyp.* Quicia.

Kinyo. Tired. *Span. Gyp.* Quiñao.

Kisaiya. A female Gypsy name.

Kisi, *ad.* How much, to what degree: kisi puro shan tu, how old are you? *Wal.* Kitze. *Span. Gyp.* Quichi. *Sans.* Kati (how many?)

Kisseh | *s.* A purse. *Sans.* Kosa. *Pers.* كيسه
Kissi |

Kistur, *v. a.* To ride. *Wal.* Keleri.

Kistri-mengro | *s.* Rider, horseman.
Kistro-mengro |

Kitchema, *s.* Public-house, inn. *Hun.* Korcsma. *Wal.* Keirtchumie.

Kitchema-mengro, *s.* Innkeeper.

Klism | *s.* A key. *Rus.* Cliotche. *Mod. Gr.* κλείσμα (shut-
Klisn | ting up).

Klism-engri, *s.* A lock. Lit. key-thing.

Klism-hev, *s.* A keyhole.

Klop, *s.* A gate, seemingly a cant word; perhaps a bell. *Wal.* Klopot.

Kokkodus. Uncle: kokkodus Artáros, Uncle Arthur.

Komi, *adv.* More: ever-komi, evermore.

Koosho, *a.* Good: kooshi gillie, a good song. *Sans.* Kusala.

Kora | *v. a.* To riot. *Wal.* Kiorei (to cry out, bawl, make a
Kore | tumult). *Heb.* Kara (he convoked, cried out).

Koring, *part. pres.* Rioting. *Heb.* Kirivah (proclamation).

Kora-mengro, *s.* A rioter.

Kore, *v. a.* To hawk goods about, to cry out, to proclaim.

Koring lil, *s.* Hawking-licence.

Koring chiriclo, *s.* The cuckoo.

Koshto, *a.* Good. *Pers.* كوست

Koshtipen, *s.* Goodness, advantage, profit: kek koshtipen in dukkering knau, it is of no use to tell fortunes now.

Kosko, *a.* Good.

Koskipen, *s.* Goodness.

Krallis, *s.* King. *Rus.* Korol. *Hun.* Király. *Wal.* Kraiu.

Kushto, *a.* Good: kushto si for mangui, I am content.

L

La, *pro. pers.* Her; accusative of 'i' or 'yoi,' she.

Laki, *pro. poss.* Her: laki die, her mother.

Lang
Lango } *a.* Lame. *Sans.* Lang. *Pers.* لنَك Lenk.

Lasa
Lasar } With her; instrumental case of 'i.'

Lashi
Lasho } Louis. *Hungarian*, Lajos, Lazlo. *Scotch*, Lesley.

Latch, *v. a.* To find. *Wal.* Aphla.

Later. From her; ablative of 'i.'

Lati. Genitive of 'i'; frequently used as the accusative — *e.g.* cams tu lati, do you love her?

Lav, *s.* Word. *Sans.* Lapa (to speak). *Eng.* Lip.

Lavior, *pl.* Words.

Lav-chingaripen, *s.* Dispute, word-war.

Lav-engro, *s.* Word-master, linguist.

Len, *pro. pers. pl.* To them: se len, there is to them, they have.

Lendar, *ablative.* From them.

Lende
Lunde } *gen. and acc.* Of them, them.

Lensar. With them.

Lengué, *pro. poss.* Their: lengue tan, their tent.

Les, *pro. pers.* To him; dative of 'yo,' he: pawno stadj se les, he has a white hat.

Lescro, *pro. poss.* His, belonging to him: lescro prala, his brother.

Leste. Of him, *likewise* him; genitive and accusative of 'yo.'

Lester. From him.

Leste's. His: leste's wast, his hand; properly, lescro wast.

Lesti. Her *or* it: pukker zi te lesti, tell her your mind; he can't rokkra lesti, he can't speak it.

Leav | *v. a.* To take. *Wal.* Loua.
Ley |

Lel. He takes.

Lel cappi. Get booty, profit, capital.

Lennor, *s.* Summer, spring.

Levinor, *s.* Ale; drinks in which there is wormwood. *Heb.* Laenah (wormwood). *Irish*, Lion (ale).

Levinor-ker, *s.* Alehouse.

Levinor-engri. Hop. Lit. ale-thing.

Levinor-engriken tem. Kent. Lit. hop-country.

Li, *pron.* It: dovo se li, that's it.

Lidan, *v. a.* You took; *2nd pers. pret.* of Ley.

Lil, *s.* Book; a letter or pass. *Hun.* Level. *Sans.* Likh (to write). *Hindustani*, Likhan (to write).

Lillai, *s.* Summer. *Hun. Gyp.* Nilei.

Linnow, *part. pass.* Taken, apprehended.

Lis, *pro. dat.* To it: adrey lis, in it.

Lollo | *a.* Red. *Pers.* لال Lal.
Lullo |

Lolle bengres, *s. pl.* Red waistcoats, Bow Street runners.

Lollo matcho, *s.* Red herring. Lit. red fish.

Lolli plaishta, *s.* A red cloak.

Lolli, *s.* A farthing.

Lon | *s.* Salt. *Sans.* Lavana. *Hin.* Lon.
Lun |

Lou, *pro.* It: oprey-lou, upon it. *Wal.* Lou.

Loure, *v. a.* To steal. *See* Luripen.

Lubbeny, *s.* Harlot. *Rus.* Liabodieitza (adultress), liobo-deinoe (adulterous). *Sans* Lúbha (to inflame with lust, to desire). The English word Love is derived from this Sanscrit root.

Lubbenipen, *s.* Harlotry.

Lubbenified. Become a harlot.

Lundra. London. *Mod. Gr.* Λόνδρα.

Luripen, *s.* Robbery, a booty. Lit. a seizure. *Wal.* Luare (seizure, capture), Louarea Parizouloui (the capture of Paris).

Lutherum, *s.* Sleep, repose, slumber.

Luvvo, *s.* Money, currency. *Rus.* Lóvok (convenient,

handy, quick, agile). In Spanish Gypsy, a real (small coin) is called Quelati, a thing which dances, from Quelar, to dance.

Luvvo-mengro, *s.* Money-changer, banker.

Luvvo-mengro-ker, *s.* Banker's house, bank.

M

Má, *ad.* Not; only used before the imperative: má muk, let not. *Sans.* Mā. *Pers.* ؋

Maas, *s.* *Sans.* Mansa Mans. *Rus.* Maso. *See* Mas.

Mass-engro ⎱ *s.* Butcher.
Maaso-mengro ⎰

Mailla, *s.* Ass, donkey. *Wal.* Megaroul. *Sans.* Baluya.

Mailla and posh. Ass and foal.

Malleco, *a.* False.

Malúno ⎱ *s.* Lightning. *Rus.* Mólnïya.
Maloney ⎰

Mam, *s.* Mother. *Wal.* Moume. *Welsh*, Mam. *Irish and Scottish Gaelic*, Muime (a nurse).

Man, *prom. pers.* I; very seldom used. *Hin.* Muen.

Mande, *pron. pers. oblique* of Man; generally used instead of the nominative Man.

Mander. Ablative of Man, from me: jā mander, go from me.

Mande's. My. Mande's wast, my hand; used improperly for miro.

Mangue. Dative of Man, to me; sometimes used instead of the nominative.

Mansa. With me.

Mang, *v. a.* To beg. *Hin.* Mangna. *Sans.* Mārg.

Mango-mengro, *s.* A beggar.

Mangipen, *s.* The trade of begging. *Sans.* Mārgana (begging).

Manricley, *s.* A cake. *Span. Gyp.* Manricli.

Manush, *s.* Man. *Sans.* Mānasha. *Span. Gyp.* Manus. *See* Monish.

Manushi, *s.* Woman, wife. *Sans.* Manushi.

Maricli, *s.* A cake. *See* Maricley.

Mash, *s.* Umbrella. A cant word.

Matcho, *s.* A fish. *Sans.* Matsya. *Hin.* Muchee.

Matcheneskoe Gav. Yarmouth. Lit. the fishy town.

Matcheneskoe guero, *s.* A fisherman.

Matchka, *s. f.* A cat. *Hun*. Macska.

Matchko, *s. m.* A he-cat.

Mattipen, *s.* Drunkenness. *Sans* Matta (to be intoxicated). *Mod. Gr.* Μέθη (intoxication). *Welsh*, Meddwy (to intoxicate).

Matto, *a.* Drunk, intoxicated. *Welsh*, Meddw.

Matto-mengro, *s.* Drunkard.

Mea, *s.* Mile: dui mear, two miles. *Wal* Mie.

Mea-bar, *s.* Milestone.

Medisin, *s.* Measure, bushel. *Sans*. Māna.

Mek, *v. n.* Leave, let: meklis, leave off, hold your tongue, have done. *Sans* Moksh.

Men, *pr.* We; pl. of Man.

Men, *s.* Neck. *Gaelic*, Muineal. *Welsh*, Mwng. *Mandchou* Meifen.

Men-pangushi, *s.* Neckcloth. *See* Pangushi.

Mengro. A word much used in composition. *See* Engro and Mescro.

Mensalli, *s.* A table. *Wal*. Masi.

Mer ⎱ *v. n.* To die. *Sans*. Mri.
Merava ⎰

Merricley, *s.* A cake. *See* Manricley.

Merripen, *s.* Death. *Sans*. Mara.

Merripen, *s.* Life, according to the Gypsies, though one feels inclined to suppose that the real signification of the word is Death; it may, however, be connected with the Gaulic or Irish word Mairam, to endure, continue, live long: Gura' fada mhaireadh tu! may you long endure, long life to you! In Spanish Gypsy Merinao signifies an immortal.

Mescro. A *particle* which, affixed to a verb, forms a substantive masculine: — *e.g.* Camo, I love; camo-mescro, a lover. Nash, to run; nashi-mescro, a runner. It is equivalent to Mengro, *q.v.*

Messalli, *s.* A table. *Wal*. Masi.

Mestipen, *s.* Life, livelihood, living, fortune, luck, goodness. *Span. Gyp.* Mestipen, bestipen. *Wal.* Viatsie.

Mi, *pron.* I, my.

Mi cocoro, *prom. poss.* I myself, I alone.

Mi dearie Dubbeleskey. For my dear God's sake.

Mi develeskie gueri, *s. f.* A holy female.

Mi develeskie gueri Mary. Holy Virgin Mary.

Mi develeskoe Baval Engro. Holy Ghost.

Mi dubbelungo, *a.* Divine.

Mi duvvelungo divvus, *s.* Christmas Day.

Millior, *s.* Miles; panj millior, five miles.

Minge }
Mintch } *s.* Pudendum muliebre.

Miro, *pron. poss.* My, mine.

Miri, *pron. poss. f.* My, mine.

Misto }
Mistos } *ad.* Well.

Misto dusta. Very well.

Mistos amande. I am glad.

Mitch, *s. See* Minge.

Mizella. Female Gypsy name.

Mokkado, *a.* Unclean to eat. *Wal.* Mourdar (dirty).

Monish, *s.* Man. *See* Manush.

Mol, *s.* Wine. *See* Mul.

Mollauvis, *s.* Pewter.

Moomli, *s.* Candle, taper. *See* Mumli.

Moomli-mengro, *s.* Candlestick, lantern.

Moar, *v. a.* To grind. *See* Morro.

More }
Morava } *v. a.* To kill, slay. *Sans.* Mri. *Wal.* Omori.

Moreno, *part. pass.* Killed, slain.

More, *v. a.* To shave, shear. *Hun. Gyp.* Murinow.

Mormusti, *s.f.* Midwife. *Wal.* Maimoutsi. *Rus.* Mameichka
(nurse).

Moro, *pron. poss.* Our: moro dad, our father.

Morro, *s.* Bread. Lit. that which is ground. *See* Moar.
Span. Gyp. Manro. *Hun. Gyp.* Manro, also Gheum: sin
gheum manro, gheum is manro (bread). *Rus. Gyp.*
Morroshka (a loaf).

Morro-mengro, *s.* A baker.

Mort, *s.* Woman, concubine; a cant word.

Mosco }
Moshko } A fly. *Lat.* Musca. *Wal.* Mouskie. *Span. Gyp.*
Moscabis (fly-blown, stung with love, picado,
enamorado).

Moskey, *s.* A spy: to jal a moskeying, to go out spying. *Fr.*
Mouchard.

Mufta, *s. f.* Box, chest. *See* Muktar.

Mui, *s.* Face, mouth: lollo leste mui, his face is red. *Sans.*
Mukha (face, mouth). *Fr.* Mot (a word). *Provenzal*,
Mo.

Muk, *v. n.* To leave, let. *See* Mek.

Mukkalis becunye. Let it be.

Muktar | *s.* Box, chest
Mukto |

Mul, *s.* Wine. *Pers.* Mul.

Mul divvus. Christmas Day. Lit. wine day.

Mul-engris, *s. pl.* Grapes: mul-engri tan, vineyard.

Mulleni muktar, *s.* Coffin. Lit. dead-chest.

Mullodustie mukto. *Id.*

Mulleno hev, *s.* Grave.

Mulleno kêr, *s.* Sepulchre, cemetery.

Mullo, *s., a.* Dead man, dead.

Mullo mas, *s.* Dead meat; flesh of an animal not slain, but
which died alone.

Mumli, *s. f.* Candle.

Mumli-mescro, *s.* Chandler.

Munjee, *s.* A blow on the mouth, seemingly a cant word.
Hin. Munh, mouth. *Ger.* Mund.

Murces | *s. pl.* Arms. *Span. Gyp.* Murciales.
Mursior |

Muscro, *s.* Constable. *See* Muskerro.

Mush, *s.* Man. *Rus.* Mouge. *Finnish*, Mies. *Tibetian*, Mi.
Lat. Mas (a male).

Mushi, *s.* Woman.

Mushipen, *s.* A little man, a lad. *Toulousian*, Massip (a
young man), massipo (a young woman).

Muskerro, *s.* Constable.

Muskerriskoe cost, *s.* Constable's staff.

Mutra, *s.* Urine.

Mutrava, *v. a.* To void urine. *Sans.* Mutra.

Mutra-mengri, *s.* Tea.

Mutzi, *s.* Skin. *Span. Gyp.* Morchas.

Mutzior, *s. pl.* Skins.

Na, *ad.* Not.

Naflipen, *s.* Sickness. *Span. Gyp.* Nasallipen. *Mod. Gr.* νόσευμα.

Naflo, *a.* Sick.

Nai. Properly Na hi, there is not: nai men chior, we have no girls.

Naior, *s. pl.* Nails of the fingers or toes. *Mod. Gr.* νύχι.

Nangipen, *s.* Nakedness.

Nango, *s.* Naked.

Narilla } A female Gypsy name.
Narrila }

Nash, *v. a.* To run. *Span. Gyp.* Najar.

Nashimescro, *s.* Runner, racer.

Nashimescro-tan, *s.* Race-course.

Nash, *v. a.* To lose, destroy, to hang. *Sans* Nasa. *Span. Gyp.* Najabar (to lose). *Sans.* Nakha (to destroy). *Eng.* Nacker (a killer of old horses).

Nashado, *part. pret.* Lost, destroyed, hung.

Nashimescro, *s.* Hangman.

Nashko, *part. pass.* Hung: nashko pré rukh, hung on a tree.

Nasho, *part. pass.* Hung.

Nástis, *a.* Impossible. *See* Astis.

Nav, *s.* Name. *Hun.* Nev.

Naval, *s.* Thread. *Span. Gyp.* Nafre.

Naes } *postpos.* According to, after the manner of: gorgiko-
Nes } naes, after the manner of the Gentiles; Romano-chalugo-naes, after the manner of the Gypsies.

Ne, *ad.* No, not: ne burroder, no more; ne riddo, not dressed.

Nevo, *a.* New.

Nevi, *a. fem.* New: nevi tud from the guveni, new milk from the cow.

Nevey Rukhies. The New Forest. Lit. new trees.

Nevi Wesh. The New Forest.

Nick, *v. a.* To take away, steal. *Span. Gyp.* Nicabar.

Nick the cost. To steal sticks for skewers and linen-pegs.

Nogo, *s.* Own, one's own; nogo dad, one's own father; nogo tan, one's own country.

Nok, *s.* Nose. *Hin.* Nakh.

Nok-engro, *s.* A glandered horse. Lit. a nose-fellow.
Nokkipen, *s.* Snuff.

O

O, *art. def.* The.
O, *pron.* He.
Odoi, *ad.* There. *Hun.* Ott, oda.
Oduvvu, *pron. dem.* That. *Span. Gyp.* Odoba.
Olevas ⎫
Olivas ⎬ *s. pl.* Stockings. *Span. Gyp.* Olibias. *Wal.*
Olivor ⎭   Chorapul.
Opral ⎫
Opré ⎬ *prep.* Upon, above. *Wal.* Pre, asoupra.
Oprey ⎭
Or. A plural termination; for example, Shock, a cabbage,
    pl. shock-or. It is perhaps derived from Ouri, the plural
    termination of Wallachian neuter nouns ending in 'e.'
Ora, *s. f.* A watch. *Hun.* Ora.
Ora, *s.* An hour: so si ora, what's o'clock?
Orlenda. Gypsy female name. *Rus.* Orlitza (female eagle).
Os. A common termination of Gypsy nouns. It is frequently
    appended by the Gypsies to English nouns in order to
    disguise them.
Owli, *ad.* Yes. *See* Avali.

P

Pa, *prep.* By: pá mui, by mouth. *Rus.* Po.
Padlo, *ad.* Across: padlo pawnie, across the water, trans-
    ported.
Pahamengro, *s.* Turnip.
Pailloes, *s.* Filberts.
Pal, *s.* Brother.
Pal of the bor. Brother of the hedge, hedgehog.
Palal, *prep. ad.* Behind, after, back again: av palal, come
    back, come again: palal the welgorus, after the fair. *Mod.*
    Gr. πάλιν (again). *Rus.* Opiat *(id.)*.
Pali, *ad.* Again, back.

Pand, *v. a.* To bind. *Sans.* Bandh.

Pandipen, *s.* Pinfold, prison, pound.

Pandlo, *part. pass.* Bound, imprisoned, pounded.

Pand opre, *v. a.* To bind up.

Pandlo-mengro, *s.* Tollgate, thing that's shut.

Pangushi, *s. f.* Handkerchief.

Pāni, *s.* Water. *See* Pawni.

Pānishey shock, *s.* Watercress. Lit. water-cabbage. *See* Shok.

Panj, *a.* Five. *See* Pansch.

Pani-mengro, *s.* Sailor, waterman.

Panni-mengri, *s.* Garden.

Panno, *s.* Cloth. *Lat.* Pannus. *Wal.* Penzie.

Pansch, *s.* Five. *Hin.* Panch.

Pappins ⎫
Pappior ⎭ *s. pl.* Ducks. *Mod. Gr.* πάπια.

Paracrow, *v. a.* To thank: paracrow tute, I thank you.

Parava ⎫
Parra ⎭ *v. a.* To change, exchange. *See* Porra.

Parriken, *s.* Trust, credit. *Mod. Gr.* παρακαταθήκη (trusted goods).

Parno, *a.* White. *See* Pauno.

Pas, *s.* Half. *See* Posh.

Pasherro, *s.* Halfpenny; *pl.* pasherie. *Pers.* پاشيز Pasheez (a farthing).

Pas-more, *v. a.* Half-kill.

Patch, *s.* Shame. *Span. Gyp.* Pachi, modesty, virginity. *Sans.* Putchā.

Patnies, *s. pl.* Ducks.

Patrin, *s.* A Gypsy trail; handfuls of leaves or grass cast by the Gypsies on the road, to denote to those behind the way which they have taken.

Pattin, *s.* A leaf. *Span. Gyp.* Patia. *Sans.* Patra.

Pattinor. Leaves.

Paub ⎫
Paubi ⎭ *s.* An apple. *Hung. Gyp.* Paboy.

Paub tan, *s.* Orchard.

Pauno, *a.* White. *Sans.* Pandu. *Gaelic*, Ban.

Pauno gad. Clean shirt.

Pauno sherro. Grey head, white head.

Pauno, *s.* Flour. Lit. what is white. The Latin 'panis' seems to be connected with this word.

Pauno-mengro, *s.* A miller, white fellow.

Pauno-mui, *s.* Pale face; generally applied to a vain, foolish girl, who prefers the company of the pallid Gentiles to that of the dark Romans.

Pauvi, *s.* An apple.

Pauvi-pāni, *s.* Cyder, apple-water.

Pawdel, *ad.* Across, over: pawdel puve and pawni, across land and water; pawdel the chumba, over the hill.

Pawnee ⎱ *s.* Water. *Sans.* Pāniya. *Hin.* 'Panie. *Eng.* Pond.
Pawni ⎰   *See* Pāni.

Pawnugo, *a.* Watery: pawnugo hev, water-hole, well.

Pazorrhus, *part. pass.* Indebted. *See* Pizarris.

Péava, *v. a.* To drink. *Sans.* Pā.

Péa-mengri, *s.* Tea-pot. *Wal.* Bea. *Lit.* drinking thing.

Peeapen, *s.* Health: ako's your peeapen! here's your health!

Pea-mengro, *s.* Drunkard.

Pedloer, *s.* Nuts; *prop.* Acorns. *Pers.* Peleed.

Peerdie, *s.* Female tramper.

Peerdo, *s.* Male tramper.

Pek'd ⎱ *part. pass.* Roasted. *Span. Gyp.* Peco. *Sans.* Pāka
Pekt ⎰   (cooking). *Pers.* Pekhtan. *Rus.* Petsch (oven).

Pele, *s. pl.* Testicles. *Sans.* P'hala.

Pelengo gry ⎱ *s.* Stone-horse.
Pelengro gry ⎰

Pen, a *particle* affixed to an adjective or a verb when some property or quality, affection or action is to be expressed, the termination of the first word being occasionally slightly modified: for example, Kosko, good, koskipen, goodness; Tatcho, true, tatchipen, truth; Camo, I love, camipen, love; Chingar, to fight, chingaripen, war. It is of much the same service in expressing what is abstract and ideal as Engro, Mescro, and Engri are in expressing what is living and tangible. It is sometimes used as a diminutive, *e.g.* Mushipen, a little fellow.

Pen, *s.* Sister.

Pen ⎱ *v. a.* To say, speak. *Wal.* Spoune.
Penav ⎰

Penchava, *v. n.* To think. *Pers.* Pendashten. *Sans.* Vi-cit.

Penliois, *s.* Nuts. *See* Pedloer.

Per, *s.* Belly.

Per, *v. n.* To fall. *Span. Gyp.* Petrar. *Sans*. Pat.

Per tuley. To fall down.

Perdo, *a.* Full. *Sans*. Purva, to fill.

Pes   ⎧ *v. a.* To pay. *Span. Gyp.* Plaserar. *Rus.* Platit. *Wal.*
Pessa ⎰   Pleti. *Hun.* Fizetni.

Pes apopli. To repay.

Petul, *s.* A horse-shoe. *Mod. Gr.* πέταλον. *Wal.* Potkoavie. *Heb.* Bedel (tin).

Petul-engro, *s.* Horseshoe-maker, smith, tinker; the name of a Gypsy tribe.

Pi, *v. a.* To drink. *Sans*. Piva (drinking). *See* Peava.

Pias, *s.* Fun. *Mod. Gr.* παίζω (to play).

Pikkis   ⎧ *s. pl.* Breasts. *See* Birk, bark. *Wal.* Piept.
Pikkaris ⎰

Pikko, *s.* Shoulder.

Pios, *part. pass.* Drunken. Only employed when a health is drunk: *e.g.* aukko tu pios adrey Romanes, your health is drunk in Romany.

Píre, *s. pl.* Feet.

Pirè, *s. pl.* Trampers.

Pire-gueros, *s. pl.* Travellers, trampers. Lit. foot-fellows.

Pireni, *s. f.* Sweetheart.

Pireno, *s. m.* Sweetheart.

Piro, *v. a.* To walk: pirel, he walks.

Piro-mengro, *s.* Walker.

Pirry, *s.* Pot, boiler. This is a west-country Gypsy word. *Span. Gyp.* Piri. *Sans*. Pithara, pātra.

Pishen, *s.* Flea, any kind of insect: guldo pishen, honey-insect, bee, honey.

Pivli, *s.* A widow.

Pivlo, *s.* A widower.

Pivley-gueri, *s.* A widowed female.

Pivley-guero, *s.* A widowed fellow.

Pivley-raunie, *s.* A widow lady.

Piya-mengro, *s.* Drunkard. *See* Pea-mengro.

Pizarris   ⎧ *part. pass.* Trusted, credited, in debt. *Sans*.
          ⎪ Vishvas (to trust). *Wal.* Se bizoui (to trust, to
Pizaurus ⎨ credit). *Mod. Gr.* πιστευθίες (he who has
          ⎪ been credited). *Span. Gyp.* Bisarar (to owe),
          ⎩ bisauras (debts), pista (an account).

Pizarri-mengro, *s.* A trusted person, a debtor.

Plakta, *s.* Sheet: bero-rukiskie plakta, a ship's sail.

Plashta, *s.* Cloak: lolli plashta, red cloak. *Span. Gyp.* Plata.
Plakta and plashta are probably both derived from the
Wallachian postat, a sheet.

Plastra, *v. a.* To run.

Plastra lesti. Run it; run for your life.

Plastra-mengro, *s. a.* A Bow Street runner, a pursuer. In
Spanish Gypsy, Plastañi means a company which
pursues robbers.

Poggado, *part. pass.* Broken.

Poggado bavol-engro, *s.* Broken-winded horse.

Poggado habben, *s.* Broken victuals.

Poggra, *v. a.* To break. *Wal.* Pokni.

Poggra-mengri, *s.* A mill. Lit. a breaking thing.

Poknies, *s.* Justice of the peace. *Rus.* Pokoio (to pacify).

Pokiniskoe ker, *s.* House of a justice of the peace.

Pooshed *part. pass.* Buried: mulo ta poosheno, dead and
Poosheno   buried.

Por, *s.* Feather. *Pers.* Par. *Sans.* Parna.

Por-engro, *s.* Pen-master, penman, one able to write.

Por-engri-pen, *s.* Penmanship, writing.

Porior, *s. pl.* Feathers.

Pordo, *a.* Heavy. *Wal.* Povarie (a weight). *Lat.* Pondus.

Porra, *v. a.* To exchange.

Posh, *s.* Half.

Posherro
Poshoro *s.* Halfpenny.

Possey-mengri, *s.* Pitchfork; improperly used for any fork.
The literal meaning is a straw-thing; a thing used for the
removal of straw. *See* Pus.

Potan, *s.* Tinder. *Wal.* Postabh (sheet, cloth). *Sans.* Pata
(cloth).

Poov
Pov *s.* Earth, ground. *Sans.* Bhu.

Poov, *v.* To poov a gry, to put a horse in a field at night.

Pov-engro, *s.* An earth thing, potato.

Pov-engreskoe, *a.* Belonging to the potato.

Povengreskoe gav. Potato town — Norwich.

Povengreskoe tem. Potato country — Norfolk.

Povo-guero, *s.* Mole, earth-fellow.

Praio, *a.* Upper: praio tem, upper country, heaven. *Span.*

Gyp. Tarpe (heaven). *See* Opré.

Prala, *s.* Brother.

Pude, *v. a.* To blow.

Pude-mengri, *s.* Blowing thing, bellows.

Pudge, *s.* Bridge. *Wal.* Pod, podoul. *Pers.* Pul. *Sans.* Pāli.

Pukker, *v. a.* To tell, declare, answer, say, speak. *Span.*
    Gyp. Pucanar (to proclaim). *Hin.* Pukar, pukarnar.

Pur, *s.* Belly. *See* Per.

Pureno, *a.* Ancient, old: pureno foky, the old people. *Sans.*
    Purvya (ancient).

Puro, *a.* Old. *Sans.* Purā.

Puro dad, *s.* Grandfather.

Purrum, *s.* Leek, onion. *Lat.* Porrum.

Purrum   *n. pr.* Lee, or Leek; the name of a numerous
Purrun   Gypsy tribe in the neighbourhood of London.
        Wal. Pur (onion). *Lat.* Porrum. *Sans.* Purāna
        (ancient).

Pus, *s.* Straw. *Sans.* Busa, chaff.

Putch, *v. a.* To ask. *Hin.* Puchhna.

Putsi, *s.* Purse, pocket. *Sans.* Putā, pocket. *Wal.* Pountsi.
    Old cant, Boung.

Putsi-lil, *s.* Pocket-book.

Puvvo, *s.* Earth, ground. *See* Poov.

Puvvesti churi, *s. a.* Plough.

R

Raia, *s.* Gentleman, lord. *See* Rye.

Rak, *v. n.* To beware, take care; rak tute, take care of
    yourself. *Sans.* Raksh (to guard, preserve).

Rakli, *s. f.* Girl.

Raklo, *s.* Boy, lad.

Ran, *s.* Rod: ranior, rods. *Sans.* Ratha (cane, ratan).

Rarde, *s.* Night. *Sans* Rātri.

Rardiskey, *a.* Nightly.

Rardiskey kair poggring, *s.* Housebreaking by night,
    burglary.

Rashengro, *s.* Clergyman.

Rashi, *s.* Clergyman, priest. *Sans.* Rishi (holy person).

Rashieskey rokkring tan, *s.* Pulpit.

Ratcheta, *s.* A goose, duck. *See* Retsa.

Ratti, *s.* Blood. *Sans.* Rudhira.

Ratniken chiriclo, *s.* Nightingale.

Rawnie, *s.* Lady.

Rawniskie dicking gueri, *s.* Lady-like looking woman.

Rawniskie tatti naflipen, *s.* The lady's fever, maladie de France.

Retza, *s.* Duck. *Wal.* Rierzoiou. *See* Rossar-mescro. *Hun.* Récze.

Reyna. A female Gypsy name.

Riddo, *part. pass.* Dressed. *Span. Gyp.* Vriardao.

Rig ⎫
Riggur ⎬ *v. a.* To bear, carry, bring.
Riggurava ⎭

Rig in zi. To remember, bear in mind.

Rig to zi. To bring to mind.

Rinkeno, *a.* Handsome.

Rivipen, *s.* Dress. Lit. linen clothes, women's dress. *Wal.* Ruphe. *Mod. Gr.* ῥάπτης (a tailor). In Spanish Gypsy clothes are called Goneles, from the Wallachian Khainele.

Rodra, *v. a.* To search, seek.

Roi, *s.* Spoon.

Rokra, *v. a.* To talk, speak. *Rus.* Rek (he said). *Lat.* Loquor.

Rokrenchericlo, *s.* Parrot, magpie.

Rokrenguero, *s.* A lawyer, talker. *Gaelic*, Racaire (a chatterer).

Rokrengueriskey gav. Talking fellows' town — Norwich.

Rokunyes, *s.* Trousers, breeches. *Hun. Gyp.* Roklia (gown). *Mod. Gr.* ῥόχον (cloth).

Rom, *s.* A husband. *Sans.* Rama (a husband), Rama (an incarnation of Vishnu), Rum (to sport, fondle). *Lat.* Roma (City of Rama). *Gaelic*, Rom (organ of manhood). *Eng.* Ram (aries, male sheep). *Heb.* Ream (monoceros, unicorn).

Rommado, *part. pass. s.* Married, husband.

Romm'd, *part. pass.* Married.

Romano Chal ⎫
Romany Chal ⎬ A Gypsy fellow, Gypsy lad. *See* Chal.

Romani chi. Gypsy lass, female Gypsy.

Romanes � Gypsy language.
Romany ⎦

Romaneskoenaes. After the Gypsy fashion. *Wal.*
Roumainesk (Roumainean, Wallachian.)

Romano Rye � Gypsy gentleman.
Romany Rye ⎦

Romipen, *s.* Marriage.

Rook � *s.* Tree. *Sans.* Vriksha. *Hun. Gyp.* Rukh. *Span.*
Rukh ⎦ *Gyp.* Erucal (an *olive*-tree).

Rookeskey cost. Branch of a tree.

Rooko-mengro, *s.* Squirrel. Lit. tree-fellow.

Roshto, *a.* Angry. *Wal.* Resti (to be angry).

Rossar-mescro, *s.* Gypsy name of the tribe Heron, or
Herne. Lit. duck-fellow.

Roujiou, *a.* Clean. *See* Iuziou.

Rove, *v. n.* To weep. *Sans.* Rud.

Rup, *s.* Silver. *Sans.* Raupya. *Hin.* Rupee.

Rupenoe, *a.* Silver: rupenoe péa-mengri, silver tea-pots.

Ruslipen, *s.* Strength.

Ruslo, *a.* Strong. *Mod. Gr.* ῥῶσω (roborabo). *Rus.* Rusluy
(great, huge of stature). *Hun.* Erö (strength), erös
(strong).

Rye, *s.* A lord, gentleman. *Sans.* Raj, Rayā.

Ryeskoe, *a.* Gentlemanly.

Ryeskoe dicking guero. Gentlemanly looking man.

Ryoriskey rokkaring keir, *s.* The House of Commons. Lit.
the gentleman's talking house.

S

Sacki. Name of a Gypsy man.

Sainyor, *s.* Pins. *Span. Gyp.* Chingabar (a pin).

Sal, *v. n.* To laugh; properly, he laughs. *Span. Gyp.*
Asaselarse. *Sans.* Has.

Salla. She laughs.

Salivaris, *s. f.* Bridle. *See* Sollibari.

Sap ⎤ *s.* Snake, serpent. *Wal* Sharpelé. *Span. Gyp.*
Sarp ⎦ Chaplesca.

Sappors, *s. pl.* Snakes.

Sap drey chaw. A snake in the grass: sap drey bor, a snake in the hedge.

Sapnis, *s.* Soap. *Mod. Gr. σαποῦνι. Wal.* Sipoun.

Sar, *postpos., prepos.* With: mensar, with us; sar amande, with me.

Sar, *conjunct.* As.

Sar, *ad.* How.

Sar shin, How are you? Sar shin, meero rye? Sar shin meeri rawnie? How are you, sir? How are you madam?

Sas. If it were. *See* Is.

Sas, *s.* Nest. *See* Tass.

Sarla, *s.* Evening: koshti sarla, good evening. *See* Tasarla. *Wal.* Seara. *Mod Gr. σίδηρον.*

Saster, *s.* Iron.

Saster-mengri, *s.* A piece of iron worn above the knee by the skewer-makers whilst engaged in whittling.

Saster-mengro, *s.* Ironmonger.

Sasters, sastris. Nails: chokkiskey sastris, shoe-nails.

Sau, *adv.* How.

Sau kisi. How much?

Saulohaul
Sovlehaul } *v. a.* To swear.

Saulohaul bango. To swear falsely.

Sauloholomus, *s.* Oath. *Span. Gyp.* Solája (a curse). *Arab.* صلاة Salat (prayer). *Lat.* Solemnis. *Fr.* Serment. *Wal.* Jourimint (oath).

Savo, *pron.* Who, that, which.

Saw, *v. n.* I laugh. Sawschan tu, you laugh.

Scamp. Name of a small Gypsy tribe. *Sans.* Kshump (to go).

Scourdilla, *s. f.* Platter. *Lat.* Scutella.

Scunyes
Scunyor } *s. pl.* Pins, skewers. *See* Escunyes.

Se, *3rd pers. sing. pres.* Is, there is: kosko guero se, he is a good fellow; se les, there is to him, he has.

Shab, *v. a.* Cut away, run hard, escape. *Hun.* Szabni. This word is chiefly used by the tobair coves, or vagrants.

Shan. You are, they are. *See* Shin.

Shauvo, *v.* To get with child. *See* Shuvvli.

Shehaury. Sixpence. *See* Shohaury.

Shello, *s.* Rope. *Span. Gyp.* Jele.

Shello-hokta-mengro, s. Rope-dancer.

Sher-engro, s. A head-man, leader of a Gypsy tribe.

Sher-engri, s. A halter.

Shero, s. A head. *Pers.* ﺳﺮ

Sherro's kairipen, s. Learning, head-work.

Sheshu, s. Hare, rabbit. *See* Shoshoi.

Sherrafo, a. Religious, converted. *Arab.* Sherif.

Shillenc ⎫
Shilleró ⎬ a. Cold: shillo chik, cold ground.
Shillo ⎭

Shillipen, s. Cold.

Shin. Thou art: sar shin, how art thou?

Sho, s. Thing.

Sho, a. Six.

Shohaury, s. Sixpence.

Shok, s. Cabbage: shockor, cabbages. *Span. Gyp.* Chaja.

Shom, v. *1st pers. pres.* I am. Used in the pure Roman tongue to express necessity: *e.g.* shom te jav, I must go. *Lat.* Sum. *Hun. Gyp.* Hom.

Shoob, s. Gown. *Rus.* Shoob. *See* Shubbo.

Shoon, v. n. To hear. *Pers.* Shiniden. *Sans.* Sru.

Shoonaben, s. Hearing, audience. To lel shoonaben of the covar, to take hearing of the matter.

Shoshoi, s. A hare or rabbit, but generally used by the Gypsies for the latter. *Sans.* Sasa (a hare or rabbit). *Hun. Gyp.* Shoshoi.

Shubbo, s. A gown. *Rus.* Shoob. *Wal.* Djoube.

Shubley patnies, s. pl. Geese.

Shuri. A female Gypsy name.

Shuvvali, a. Enceinte, with child.

Si, *3rd pers. sing. pres.* It is, she is; tatchipen si, it is truth; coin si rawnie, who is the lady? sossi your nav, what is your name?

Sicovar, ad. Evermore, eternally. *Hun. Gyp.* Sekovar.

Si covar ajaw. So it is.

Sig, ad. Quick, soon: cana sig, now soon. *Span. Gyp.* Singó. *Hun.* Sietö.

Sig, s. Haste.

Sikkér, v. a. To show: sikker-mengri, a show.

Simen, s. a. Equal, alike. *Sans.* Samāna.

Simen. We are, it is we. *Wal.* Semeina (to resemble).

Simmeno, *s.* Broth. *See* Zimmen.

Simmer, *v. a.* Pledge, pawn.

Simmery-mengré, *s. pl.* Pawnbrokers.

Sis. Thou art: misto sis riddo, thou art well dressed.

Siva, *v. a.* To sew. *Sans.* Siv.

Siva-mengri, *s.* A needle, sewing-thing.

Siva-mengri, *s.* Sempstress.

Siva-mengro, *s.* Tailor.

Skammen, *s.* Chair. *Wal.* Skaun. *Mod. Gr.* σκαμνι.

Skammen-engro, *s.* Chair-maker.

Skraunior, *s. pl.* Boots.

Slom ⎱
Slum ⎰ *v. a.* Follow, trace, track. *Rus.* Sliedovat.

Smentini, *s.* Cream. *Wal.* Zmentenie. *Rus.* Smetána.

So, *pron. rel.* Which, what: so se tute's kairing, what are
you doing?

Sollibari, *s.* Bridle. *Mod. Gr.* συλληβάρι.

Sonakey ⎱
Sonneco ⎰ *s.* Gold. *Sans.* Svarna.

Sore ⎱
Soro ⎰ *a.* All, every. *Sans.* Sarva.

Sorlo, *a.* Early. *Arab.* ⟞ Sohr, Sahr (morning, day-
break). *Wal.* Zorile.

Soro-ruslo, *a.* Almighty. Dad soro-ruslo, Father Almighty.

Se se? Who is it?

So si? What is it? So si ora, what's o'clock?

Soskey, *ad.* Wherefore, for what.

Sovaharri, *s.* Carpet, blanket.

Sove, *v. n.* To sleep. *Hun. Gyp.* Sovella (he sleeps). *Span.
Gyp.* Sobelar (to sleep). *Danish,* Sove (to sleep).

Sove tuley. To lie down.

Sovie, *s.* Needle. *See* Su.

Soving aley. Lying down to sleep.

Spikor, *s. pl.* Skewers. *Wal.* Spik.

Spinyor, *s. pl.* Carrots.

Spinyor, *s. pl.* Pins. *Span. Gyp.* Chingabar (a pin).

Stadj, *s.* Hat.

Stanya ⎱ *s.* A stable. *Hun.* Sanya. *Wal.* Staula, steiníe
Stanye ⎰ (sheepfold).

Stanya-mengro, *s.* Groom, stable-fellow.

Stardo, *part. pass.* Imprisoned.

Staripen, *s.* Prison.

Staro-mengro, *s.* Prisoner.

Stannyi } *s.* A deer.
Staunyo

Stiggur, *s.* Gate, turnpike. *Old cant*, Giger (a door).

Stiggur-engro, *s.* Turnpike-keeper.

Stor, *a.* Four.

Storey, *s.* Prisoner.

Stuggur, *s.* A stack.

Su, *s.* Needle. *Hun*. Tü.

Subie } *s.* Needle: subye ta naval, needle and thread.
Subye

Sueti, *s.* People. *Lithuanian*, Swetas.

Sungella, *v.* It stinks.

Sutta }
Suttur } *s.* Sleep. *Sans*. Subta (asleep). *Hin*. Sutta (sleep-
Sutu } ing). *Lat*. Sopitus.

Suttur-gillie, *s.* Sleep-song, Lullaby.

Swegler } *s.* Pipe.
Swingle

Syeira. A female Gypsy name.

T

Tā, *conj.* And.

Talleno, *a.* Woollen: talleno chofa, woollen or flannel petticoat.

Tan, *s.* Place, tent. *Hun*. Tanya.

Tard } *v. a.* To raise, build, pull, draw: the kair is
Tardra } tardrad opré, the house is built; tard the chaw
        opré, pull up the grass. *Hin*. Tornā (to pluck).
        Wal. Tratze. *Gaelic*, Tarruinn.

Tardra-mengre. Hop-pickers.

Tas, *s.* Cup, nest of a bird. *See* Dui tas, doo das.

Tasarla } *s.* To-morrow. Lit. to-early. *See* Sorlo.
Tasorlo

Tasarla, *s.* The evening. This word must not be confounded
with the one which precedes it; the present is derived
from the Wallachian Seari (evening), whilst the other is
from the Arabic Sohr, Sahar (morning).

Tassa-mengri, *s.* A frying-pan. *See* Tattra-mengri.

Tatchipen, *s.* Truth. *Sans.* Satyata.

Tatcho, *a.* True. *Sans.* Sat.

Tatti-pāni ⎱ *s.* Brandy. Lit. hot water.
Tatti-pauni ⎰

Tatti-pen, *s.* Heat.

Tatto, *a.* Hot, warm. *Sans.* Tapta. Tap (to be hot). *Gaelic*, Teth.

Tatto yeck, *s.* A hot un, or hot one; a stinging blow given in some very sensitive part.

Tattra-mengri, *s.* A frying-pan.

Tawno, *m.* ⎰ *a.* Little, small, tiny. *Sans.* Tarana (young).
Tawnie, *f.* ⎱ *Wal.* Tienir (young). *Lat.* Tener. *Span. Gyp.* Chinoro.

Tawnie yecks, *s. pl.* Little ones, grandchildren.

Te, *prep.* To: te lesti, to her; this word is not properly Gypsy.

Te, *conjunct.* That: te jinnen, that they may know, an optative word; O beng te poggar his men, may the devil break his neck. *Wal.* Ci.

Tel, *v. a. imp.* Hold: tel te jib, hold your tongue.

Tem, *s.* Country.

Temeskoe, *a.* Belonging to a country.

Temno, *a.* Dark. *Rus.* Temnoy. *Sans.* Tama (darkness).

Ten, *s. See* Tan.

Tikno, *s.* A child. *Mod. Gr.* τεκνον.

Tikno, *s.* Small, little. *Span. Gyp.* Chinoro. *Lat.* Tener.

Tippoty, *a.* Malicious, spiteful: tippoty drey mande, bearing malice against me.

Tiro, *pron.* Thine.

Tobbar, *s.* The *Road*; a Rapparee word. Boro-tobbar-killipen (the Game of High Toby — highway robbery). *Irish*, Tobar (a source, fountain).

Tornapo. Name of a Gypsy man.

Tororo, *s.* A poor fellow, a beggar, a tramp. *Sans.* Daridrā.

Tove, *v. a.* To wash: tovipen, washing. *Sans.* Dhav.

Toving divvus, *s.* Washing day, Monday.

Traish, *v. a.* To frighten, terrify: it traishes mande, it frightens me.

Trihool, *s.* Cross: Mi doveleskoe trihool, holy cross. *Span. Gyp.* Trijul. *Hin.* Trisool.

Trin, *a*. Three.

Tringrosh ⎱ Shilling. Lit. three groats.
Tringurushee ⎰

Tringurushengre, *s. pl.* Things costing a shilling.

Tringush, *s.* Shilling.

Trito, *a*. Third. *Sans*. Tritīya.

Trufféni. Female Gypsy name: Trufféni Kaumlo, Jack
Wardomescrés dieyas nav — Truffeni Lovel, the name of
John Cooper's mother. *Mod. Gr.* Τρυφωνία.

Truppior, *s. pl.* Stays.

Trupo, *s*. Body. *Wal*. Troup. *Rus*. Trup.

Trushni, *s.* Faggot.

Trusno, *a*. Thirsty, dry. *Sans*. Trishnaj.

Tu, *pron*. Thou: shoon tu, dieya! do thou hear, mother!

Tud, *s*. Milk. *Sans*. Duh (to milk).

Tudlo gueri. Milkmaid.

Tug, *a*. Sad, afflicted.

Tugnipen, *s.* Affliction.

Tugnis amande. Woe is me; I am sad.

Tugno, *a*. Sad, mournful.

Tulé ⎱ *prep*. Below, under: tuley the bor, under the hedge.
Tuley ⎰   *Slavonian*, dóly.

Tulipen, *s*. Fat, grease.

Tulo, *a*. Fat.

Tute, *pron*. Accusative of Tu; generally used instead of the
nominative.

Tuv, *s*. Smoke, tobacco.

Tuvalo ⎱ *a*. Smoky. *Span. Gyp*. Chibaló (a cigar).
Tuvvalo ⎰

V

Vangus, *s*. Finger. *Sans*. Angula.

Vangustri, *s*. Ring. *Sans*. Angulika, anguri. *See* Wangustri.

Vaneshu, *s*. Nothing. From the Wallachian Ba nitchi, not at
all.

Var, *s*. Flour: var-engro, a miller. *See* Waro.

Vardo, *s*. Cart. *See* Wardo.

Vassavo ⎱ *a*. Bad, evil.
Vassavy ⎰

Vast, *s.* Hand.

Vava. An *affix*, by which the future of a verb is formed as Heta-vava. It seems to be the Wallachian Wa-fi, he shall or will be.

Vellin, *s.* A bottle.

Vauros, *s.* A city. *Hun.* Város. *Sans.* Puri. *Hin.* Poor. *Wal.* Orash.

Vénor | Bowels, entrails. *See* Wendror.
Vennor |

W

Wafo, *a.* Another. *Sans.* Apara.

Wafo divvus, *s.* Yesterday. Lit. the other day.

Wafo tem. Another country, foreign land.

Wafo temeskoe mush, *s.* A foreigner, another countryman.

Wafo tem-engre. Foreigners.

Wafodu | *a.* Bad, evil.
Wafudo |

Wafodúder. Worse: wafodúder than dovor, worse than they.

Wafodu-pen, *s.* Wickedness.

Wafodu guero, *s.* The Evil One, Satan.

Wafodu tan, *s.* Hell, bad place.

Wangar, *s.* Coals, charcoal. *Sans.* Angara. *See* Wongar.

Wangustri, *s.* Ring.

Warda, *v.* To guard, take care: warda tu coccorus, take care of yourself.

Wardo, *s.* Cart. *Sans.* Pattra.

Wardo-mescro, *s.* Carter, cartwright, cooper, name of a Gypsy tribe.

Waro, *s.* Flour.

Waro-mescro, *s.* Miller.

Wast, *s.* Hand. *See* Vast. Wastrors, hands. *Gaelic*, Bas (the palm of the hand).

Weggaulus |
Welgorus | *s.* A fair. *Wal.* Bieltchiou.
Welgaulus |

Wel, *v. a.* He comes; from Ava. Sometimes used imperatively; *e.g.* Wel adrey, come in.

Welling páli. Coming back, returning from transportation.

Wen *s*. Winter.

Wendror, *s*. *pl*. Bowels, inside. *Wal*. Pentetche. *Lat*.
  Venter.

Wentzelow. Name of a Gypsy man.

Werriga, *s*. Chain. *Rus*. Veriga. *Wal*. Verigie (bolt).

Wesh, *s*. Forest, wood. *Pers*. شّه

Wesh-engro, *s*. Woodman, gamekeeper.

Weshen-juggal, *s*. Fox. Lit. dog of the wood.

Woddrus ⌈*s*. Bed. *Hun. Gyp*. Patos. *Wal*. Pat. The Spanish
Wuddrus ⌊   Gypsies retain the pure Indian word Charipé.

Wongar, *s*. Coal. Also a term for money; probably because
  Coal in the cant language signifies money. *See* Wangar.

Wongar-camming mush, *s*. A miser. Lit. one who loves
  coal.

Wuddur, *s*. Door. *Span. Gyp*. Burda. *Wal*. Poartie.

Wuddur-mescro, *s*. Doorkeeper.

Wust, *v. a*. To cast, throw.

Wusto-mengro, *s*. Wrestler, hurler.

Y

Yack, *s*. Eye. *Sans*. Akshi. *Germ*. Auge. *Rus*. Oko
  Lithuanian, Akis. *Lat*. Oculus.

Yackor. Eyes.

Yag, *s*. Fire. *Sans*. Agni. *Rus*. Ogon. *Lithuanian*, Ugnis
  Lat. Ignis. *Irish*, An (water, fire).

Yag-engri, *s*. Gun, fire-thing.

Yag-engro ⌉*s*. Gamekeeper, sportsman, fireman.
Yago-mengro ⌋

Yag-kairepénes, *s*. Fireworks.

Yag-vardo, *s*. Fire-car, railroad carriage.

Yarb, *s*. Herb.

Yarb-tan, *s*. Garden.

Yeck, *a*. One. *Sans*. Eka. *Hin*. Yak.

Yeckoro, *a*. Only: yeckoro chavo, only son.

Yeckorus, *ad*. Once.

Yo, *pron*. He.

Yoi, *pron*. She. Sometimes used for La or Las, her; *e.g.*
  Mande putch'd yoi, I asked *she*, her.

Yokki, *a*. Clever, expert: a yokki juva, a yokki woman — a

female expert at filching, ringing the changes, telling
fortunes, and other Gypsy arts. *Sans*. Yoga (artifice,
plan), Yuj (to combine, put together, plan).

Yora, *s*.   Hour. *See* Ora.

Yoro, *s*.   An egg. *Wal*. Ou.

Z

Zi, *s*.   The heart, mind. *Hun*. Sziv. *Sans*. Dhi.

Zimmen, *s*.   Broth. *Wal*. Zmenteni (cream).

Zoomi, *s. f.*   Broth, soup. *Mod. Gr.* ζουμι. *Wal*. Zamie
(juice).

Zingaro.   A Gypsy, a person of mixed blood, one who
springs from various races, a made-up person. *Sans*.
Sangkara, compositus (made-up).

Rhymed List of Gypsy Verbs

To dick and jin,
To bikn and kin;
To pee and hal,
And av and jal;
To kair and poggra,
Shoon and rokra;
To caur and chore,
Heta and cour,
Moar and more,
To drab and dook,
And nash on rook;
To pek and tove,
And sove and rove,
And nash on poove;
To tardra oprey,
And chiv aley;
To pes and gin,
To mang and chin,
To pootch and pukker,
Hok and dukker;
To besh and kel,
To del and lel,
And jib to tel;
Bitch, atch, and hatch,
Roddra and latch;
To gool and saul,
And sollohaul;
To pand and wustra,
Hokta and plastra,
Busna and kistur,

Maila and grista;
To an and riggur;
To pen and sikker,
Porra and simmer,
Chungra and chingra,
Pude and grommena,
Grovena, gruvena;
To dand and choom,
Chauva and rom,
Rok and gare,
Jib and mer
With camova,
And paracrova,
Apasavello
And mekello,
And kitsi wasror,
Sore are lavior,
For kairing chomany,
In jib of Romany.

Little Sayings

If foky kek jins bute,
Mà sal at lende;
For sore mush jins chomany
That tute kek jins.

Whatever ignorance men may show,
From none disdainful turn;
For every one doth something know
Which you have yet to learn.

BETIE ROKRAPENES

LITTLE SAYINGS

So must I ker, daiya, to ker tute mistos?

What must I do, mother, to make you well?

It is my Dovvel's kerrimus, and we can't help asarlus.

It is my God's doing, and we can't help at all.

Mi Dovvel opral, dick tuley opré mande.

My God above, look down upon me!

If I could lel bonnek tute, het-avava tute.

If I could get hold of you, I would slay you.

Misto kedast tute.

Thou hast done well.

Dovey si fino covar, ratfelo jukkal, sas miro.

That is a fine thing, you bloody dog, if it were mine.

The plastra-mengro sollohaul'd bango.

The Bow-street runner swore falsely.

Me camava jaw drey the Nevi Wesh to dick the purey Bare-mescrey.

I will go into the New Forest to see the old Stanleys.

You jin feter dovey oduvu.

You know better than that.

Will you pes for a coro levinor?

Will you pay for a pot of ale?

Mā pi kekomi.

Don't drink any more.

Mā rokra kekomi.

Do not speak any more.

Bori shil se mande.

I have a great cold.

Tatto tu coccori, pen.

Warm thyself, sister.

Kekkeno pawni dov odoi.

There is no water there.

Sore simensar si men.

We are all relations: all who are with us are ourselves.

Tatto ratti se len.

They have hot blood.

Wafudu lavior you do pen, miry deary Dovvel.

Evil words you do speak, O my dear God.

Kair pias to kair the gorgies sal.

Make fun, to make the Gentiles laugh.

Nai men chior.

I have no girls.

So se drey lis?

What is in it?

Misto sis riddo.

Thou art well dressed.

Muk man av abri.	Let me come out.
Mā kair jaw.	Don't do so.
Si covar ajaw.	The thing is so: so it is.
An men posseymengri.	Bring me a fork.
Colliko sorlo me deavlis.	To-morrow morning I will give it.
Pukker zi te lesti.	Tell her your mind.
Soving lasa.	Sleeping with her.
Tatto si can.	The sun is hot.
Mande kinyo, nastis jalno durroder.	I am tired, I can go no farther.
Mā muk de gorgey jinnen sore lidan dovvu luvvu so garridan.	Don't let the Gentiles know all the money you took which you hid.
Dui trins ta yeck ta pas.	Seven pound ten.
Pes apopli.	Pay again.
Chiv'd his vast adrey tiro putsi.	Put his hand into your pocket.
Penchavo chavo savo shan tu.	The boy is thinking who you are.
I'd sooner shoon his rokrapen than shoon Lally gil a gillie.	I would rather hear him speak than hear Lally sing.
Kekkeno jinava mande ne burreder denne chavo.	I know no more than a child.
Aukko tu pios adrey Romanes.	Here's your health in Romany!

Cotorres of Mi-Dibble's Lil Chiv'd Adrey Romanes

Pieces of Scripture Cast into Romany

THE FIRST DAY
Genesis i, 1, 2, 3, 4

Drey the sherripen Midibble kair'd the temoprey tá the puv;
    Tá the puv was chungalo, tá chichi was adrey lis;
    Tá temnopen was oprey the mui of the boro put.
    Tá Midibble's bavol-engri besh'd oprey the pánior;
    Tá Midibble penn'd: Mook there be dute! tá there was
dute.
    Tá Midibble dick'd that the doot was koosho-koshko.
    Tá Midibble chinn'd enrey the dute tá the temnopen;
    Tá Midibble kor'd the dute divvus, tá the temnopen kor'd
yo rarde;
    Tá the sarla, tá the sorlo were yeckto divvus.

THE FIFTH DAY
Genesis i, 20, 21, 22, 23

Then Midibble penn'd; Mook sore the panior
Chinn tairie jibbing engris bute dosta,
Tá prey puv be bute dosta chiricles
To vol adrey the rek of the tarpe.

Then Midibble kair'd the borie baulo-matches,
Tá sore covar that has jibbing zi adreylis,
The bute, bute tairie covars drey the panior
Sore yeck drey its genos kair'd Midibble,

The chiricles that vol adrey the tarpe
Sore yeck drey its genos kair'd he lende:
Then Midibble dick'd that sore was koosho-koshko,
And he chiv'd his koshto rokrapen opreylen:

Penn'd Midibble: Dey ye frute ever-komi,
Ever-komi be burreder your nummer,
Per with covars the panior tá durior,
Tá prey puv be burreder the chiricles!

    Then was sarla tá sorlo panschto divvus.

THE CREATION OF MAN
Genesis i, 27, 28

Then Mi-dibble kair'd Manoo drey his dikkipen
Drey Mi-dibble's dikkipen kair'd he leste;
Mush and mushi kair'd Dibble lende
And he chiv'd his koshto rokrapen opreylen:

Penn'd Mi-dibble: Dey ye frute ever-komi,
Ever-komi be burreder your nummer;
Per with chauves and chiyor the puvo
And oprey sore the puvo be krallior,

Oprey the dooiya and its matches,
And oprey the chiricles of the tarpé,
And oprey soro covar that's jibbing
And peers prey the mui of the puvo

THE LORD'S PRAYER

Meery dearie Dad, sauvo jivves drey the tem oprey, be sharrafo teero nav, te awel teero tem, be kedo sore so caumes oprey ye poov, sar kairdios drey the tem oprey. Dey man to divvus meery divvuskey morro; tá for-dey mande mande's pizzaripenes, sar mande fordeava wafor mushes lende's pizzaripenes; mā mook te petrav drey kek tentacionos, but lel mande abri from sore wafodupen; for teero se o tem, Mi-dibble, teero o ruslopen, tá yi corauni knaw tá ever-komi. Si covar ajaw.

THE APOSTLES' CREED

Apasavello drey Mi-dovel; Dad sore-ruslo savo kerdo o praio tem, tá cav acoi tulēy: tá drey lescro yekkero Chauvo Jesus Christus moro erray, beano of wendror of Mi-develeskey Geiry Mary; was curredo by the wast of Poknish Pontius Pilatos; was nash'd oprey ye Trihool; was mored, and chived adrey ye puve; jall'd tulēy ye temno drom ke wafudo tan, bengeskoe starriben; tá prey ye trito divvus jall'd yo oprey ke koshto tan, Mi-dovels ker; beshel yo knaw odoy prey Mi-dovels tatcho wast, Dad sore-ruslo; cad odoy avellava to lel shoonapen oprey jibben and merripen; Apasavello drey Mi-dibbleskey Ducos; drey the Bori Mi-develesky Bollisky Congri; that sore tatcho fokey shall jib in mestepen kettaney; that Mi-dibble will fordel sore wafudopenes; that soror mulor will jongor, and there will be kek merripen asarlus. Si covar ajaw. Avali.

The Lord's Prayer in the Gypsy Dialect of Transylvania

Miro gulo Devel, savo hal oté ando Cheros, te avel swuntunos tiro nav; te avel catari tiro tem; te keren saro so cames oppo puv, sar ando Cheros. Dé man sekhonus miro diveskoe manro, ta ierta mangue saro so na he plaskerava tuke, sar me ierstavava wafo manuschengue saro so na plaskerelen mangue. Ma muk te petrow ando chungalo camoben; tama lel man abri saro doschdar. Weika tiro sin o tem, tiri yi potea, tiri yi proslava akana ta sekovar.

Te del amen o gulo Del eg meschibo pa amara choribo.

Te vas del o Del amengue; te n'avel man pascotia ando drom, te na hoden pen mandar.

Ja Develehi!
Az Develehi!
Ja Develeskey!
Az Develeskey!
Heri Devlis!

My sweet God, who art there in Heaven, may thy name come hallowed; may thy kingdom come hither; may they do all that thou wishest upon earth, as in Heaven. Give me to-day my daily bread, and forgive me all that I cannot pay thee, as I shall forgive other men all that they do not pay me. Do not let me fall into evil desire; but take me out from all wickedness. For thine is the kingdom, thine the power, thine the glory now and ever.

May the sweet God give us a remedy for our poverty.

May God help us! May no misfortune happen to me in the road, and may no one steal anything from me.

Go with God!
Stay with God!
Go, for God's sake!
Stay, for God's sake!
By God!

Lil of Romano Jinnypen

Book of the Wisdom of the Egyptians

The tawno fokey often putches so koskipen se drey the Romano jib? Mande pens ye are sore dinneles; bute, bute koskipen se adrey lis, ta dusta, dosta of moro foky would have been bitcheno or nash'd, but for the puro, choveno Romano jib. A lav in Romany, penn'd in cheeros to a tawnie rakli, and rigg'd to the tan, has kair'd a boro kisi of luvvo and wafor covars, which had been chor'd, to be chived tuley pov, so that when the muskerres well'd they could latch vanisho, and had kek yeckly to muk the Romano they had lell'd opre, jal his drom, but to mang also his artapen.

The young people often ask: What good is there in the Romany tongue? I answers: Ye are all fools! There is plenty, plenty of good in it, and plenty, plenty of our people would have been transported or hung, but for the old, poor Roman language. A word in Romany said in time to a little girl, and carried to the camp, has caused a great purse of money and other things, which had been stolen, to be stowed underground; so that when the constables came they could find nothing and had not only to let the Gypsy they had taken up go his way, but also to beg his pardon.

His bitchenipenskie cheeros is knau abri, and it were but kosko in leste to wel keri, if it were yeckly to lel care of lescri puri, choveny romady; she's been a tatchi, tatchi romady to leste, and kek man apasavello that she has jall'd with a wafu mush ever since he's been bitcheno.

His term of transportation has now expired, and it were but right in him to come home, if it were only to take care of his poor old wife: she has been a true, true wife to him, and I don't believe that she has taken up with another man ever since he was sent across.

When yeck's tardrad yeck's beti ten oprey, kair'd yeck's beti yag anglo the wuddur, ta nash'd yeck's kekauvi by the kekauviskey saster oprey lis, yeck kek cams that a dikki-mengro or muskerro should wel and pen: so's tute kairing acai? Jaw oprey, Romano juggal.

When one's pitched up one's little tent, made one's little fire before the door, and hung one's kettle by the kettle-iron over it, one doesn't like that an inspector or constable should come and say: What are you doing here? Take yourself off, you Gypsy dog.

Prey Juliken yeckto Frydivvus, anglo nango muyiskie staunyi naveni kitchema, prey the chong opral Bororukeskoe Gav, drey the Wesh, tute dickavavasa bute Romany foky, mushor ta juvar, chalor ta cheiar.

On the first Friday of July, before the public-house called the Bald-faced Stag, on the hill above the town of the great tree in the Forest, you will see many Roman people, men and women, lads and lasses.

Jinnes tu miro puro prala Rye Stanniwix, the puro rye savo rigs a bawlo-dumo-mengri, ta kair'd desh ta stor mille barior by covar-plastring?

Do you know my old friend Mr. Stanniwix, the old gentleman that wears a pigtail, and made fourteen thousand pounds by smuggling?

He jall'd on rokkring ta rokkring dinneleskoenaes till mande pukker'd leste: if tute jasas on dovodoiskoenaes mande curavava tute a tatto yeck prey the nok.

He went on talking and talking foolishness till I said to him: If you goes on in that 'ere way I'll hit you a hot 'un on the nose.

81

You putches mande so si patrins. Patrins are Romany drom sikkering engris, by which the Romany who jal anglo muk lende that wels palal jin the drom they have jall'd by: we wusts wast-perdes of chaw oprey the puv at the jalling adrey of the drom, or we kairs sar a wangust a trihool oprey the chik, or we chins ranior tuley from the rukhies, and chivs lende oprey drey the puv aligatas the bor; but the tatcho patrin is wast-perdes of leaves, for patrin or patten in puro Romano jib is the uav of a rukheskoe leaf.

You ask me what are patrins. Patrin is the name of the signs by which the Gypsies who go before show the road they have taken to those who follow behind. We flings handfuls of grass down at the head of the road we takes, or we makes with the finger a cross-mark on the ground, or we sticks up branches of trees by the side of the hedge. But the true patrin is handfuls of leaves flung down; for patrin or patten in old Roman language means the leaf of a tree.

The tatcho drom to be a jinney-mengro is to shoon, dick, and rig in zi.

The true way to be a wise man is to hear, see, and bear in mind.

The mush savo kek se les the juckni-wast oprey his jib and his zi is keck kosko to jal adrey sweti.

The man who has not the whip-hand of his tongue and his temper is not fit to go into company.

The lil to lel oprey the kekkeno mushe's puvior and to keir the choveno foky mer of buklipen and shillipen, is wusted abri the Raioriskey rokkaring ker.

The Bill to take up the no-man's lands (commons), and to make the poor people die of hunger and cold, has been flung out of the House of Commons.

The nav they dins lati is Bokht drey Cuesni, because she rigs about a cuesni, which sore the rardies when she jals keri, is sure to be perdo of chored covars.

The name they gives her is "Luck in a basket," because she carries about a basket, which every night, when she goes home, is sure to be full of stolen property.

Cav acoi, pralor, se the nav of a lil, the sherro-kairipen of a puro kladjis of the Roumany tem. The Borobeshemescrotan, or the lav-chingaripen between ye jinneynengro ta yi sweti; or the merri-penskie rokrapen chiv'd by the zi oprey the trupo.

This here, brothers, is the title of a book, the head-work of an old king of Roumany land: the Tribunal, or the dispute between the wise man and the world: or, the death-sentence passed by the soul upon the body.

When the shello was about his men they rigg'd leste his artapen, and muk'd leste jal; but from dovo divvus he would rig a men-pangushi kek-komi, for he penn'd it rigg'd to his zee the shello about his men.

When the rope was about his neck they brought him his pardon, and let him go; but from that day he would wear a neck-kerchief no more, for he said it brought to his mind the rope about his neck.

Jack Vardomescro could del oprey dosta to jin sore was oprey the mea-bars and the drom-sikkering engris.

Jack Cooper could read enough to know all that was upon the milestones and the sign-posts.

The Romano drom to pek a chiriclo is to kair it oprey with its porior drey chik, and then to chiv it adrey the yag for a beti burroder than a posh ora. When the chik and the hatch'd porior are lell'd from the chiriclesky trupos, the per's chinn'd aley, and the wendror's wusted abri, 'tis a hobben dosta koshto for a crallissa to hal without lon.

The Roman way to cook a fowl is to do it up with its feathers in clay, and then to put it in the fire for a little more than half an hour. When the clay and the burnt feathers are taken from the fowl, the belly cut open, and the inside flung out, 'tis a food enough for a queen to eat without salt.

When Gorgio mushe's merripen and Romany Chal's merripen wels kettaney, kek kosto merripen see.

When the Gentile way of living and the Gypsy way of living come together, it is anything but a good way of living.

Yeckorus he pukker'd mande that when he was a bis beschengro he mored a gorgio, and chived the mulo mas tuley the poov; he was lell'd oprey for the moripen, but as kekkeno could latch the shillo mas, the pokiniuses muk'd him jal; he penn'd that the butsi did not besh pordo pré his zi for bute chiros, but then sore on a sudden he became tugnis and atraish of the mulo gorgio's bavol-engro, and that often of a rarde, as he was jalling posh motto from the kitchema by his cocoro, he would dick over his tatcho pikko and his bango pikko, to jin if the mulo mush's bavol-engro was kek welling palal to lel bonnek of leste.

He told me once that when he was a chap of twenty he killed a Gentile, and buried the dead meat under ground. He was taken up for the murder, but as no one could find the cold meat, the justices let him go. He said that the job did not sit heavy upon his mind for a long time, but then all of a sudden he became sad, and afraid of the dead Gentile's ghost; and that often of a night, as he was coming half-drunk from the public-house by himself, he would look over his right shoulder and over his left shoulder, to know if the dead man's ghost was not coming behind to lay hold of him.

Does tute jin the Romano drom of lelling the wast?
Avali, prala.
Sikker mande lis.
They kairs it ajaw, prala.

Do you know the Gypsy way of taking the hand?
Aye, aye, brother
Show it to me.

They does it so, brother.

A chorredo has burreder peeas than a Romany Chal.

A tramp has more fun than a Gypsy.

Tute has shoon'd the lav pazorrus. Dovodoy is so is kored
gorgikonaes "Trusted." Drey the puro cheeros the Romano
savo lelled lovvu, or wafor covars from lescro prala in
parriken, ta kek pess'd leste apopli, could be kair'd to buty for
leste as gry, mailla or cost-chinnimengro for a besh ta divvus.
To divvus kek si covar ajaw. If a Romano lelled lovvu or wafu
covars from meero vast in parriken, ta kek pessed mande
apopli, sar estist for mande te kair leste buty as gry, mailla, or
cost-chinnimengro for mande for yek divvus, kek to pen for
sore a besh?

You have heard the word pazorrus. *That is what is called
by the Gentiles "trusted," or in debt. In the old time the
Roman who got from his brother money or other things on
trust, and did not pay him again, could be made to work for
him as horse, ass, or wood cutter for a year and a day. At
present the matter is not so. If a Roman got money, or other
things, from my hand on credit, and did not repay me, how
could I make him labour for me as horse, ass, or stick-cutter
for one day, not to say for a year?*

Do you nav cavacoi a weilgorus? Ratfelo rinkeno weilgorus
cav acoi: you might chiv lis sore drey teero putsi.

*Do you call this a fair? A very pretty fair is this: you might
put it all into your pocket.*

Kek jinnipenskey covar sé to pen tute's been bango. If tute
pens tute's been bango, foky will pen: Estist tute's a koosho
koshko mushipen, but tatchipé a ratfelo dinnelo.

*It is not a wise thing to say you have been wrong. If you
allow you have been wrong, people will say: You may be a
very honest fellow, but are certainly a very great fool.*

Car's tute jibbing?
Mande's kek jibbing; mande's is atching, at the feredest; mande's a pirremengri, prala!

Where are you living?
Mind is not living; mine is staying, to say the best of it; I am a traveller, brother!

Cauna Romany foky rokkerelan yeck sar wafu penelan pal ta pen; cauna dado or deya rokkerelan ke lendes chauves penelan meero chauvo or meeri chi; or my child, gorgikonaes, to ye dui; cauna chauves rokkerelan te dad or deya penelan meero dad or meeri deya!

When Roman people speak to one another, they say brother and sister. When parents speak to their children, they say, my son, or my daughter, or my child, gorgiko-like, to either. When children speak to their parents, they say, my father, or my mother.

Meero dado, soskey were creminor kair'd? Meero chauvo, that puvo-baulor might jib by halling lende. Meero dado, soskey were puvo-baulor kair'd? Meero chauvo, that tute and mande might jib by lelling lende. Meero dado, soskey were tu ta mande kair'd? Meero chauvo, that creminor might jib by halling mende.

My father, why were worms made? My son, that moles might live by eating them. My father, why were moles made? My son, that you and I might live by catching them. My father, why were you and I made? My son, that worms might live by eating us.

Sore giv-engres shan dinneles. When they shoons a gav-engro drey the tem pen: Dov-odoy's a fino grye! they pens: Kekkeno grye se; grasni si; whether the covar's a grasni or kekkeni. Kek jinellan the dinneles that a grasni's a grye, though a grye is kek a grasni.

All farmers are fools. When they hear a citizen in the country say: That's a fine horse! they say: 'Tis no horse, 'tis a

*mare; whether the thing's a horse or not. The simpletons don't
know that a mare's a horse, though a horse is not a mare.*

Kekkeni like Romano Will's rawnie for kelling drey a
chauro.

No one like Gypsy Will's wife for dancing in a platter.

Cauna Constance Petulengri merr'd she was shel tā desch
beshor puri.

*When Constance Smith died, she was a hundred and ten
years old.*

Does tute jin Rawnie Wardomescri?
Mande jins lati misto, prala.
Does tute cam lati?
Mande cams lati bute, prala; and mande has dosta, dosta
cheeros penn'd to the wafor Romany Chals, when they were
rokkering wafudo of lati: She's a rawnie; she lels care of sore
of you; if it were kek for lati, you would sore jal to the beng.
So kerella for a jivipen?
She dukkers, prala; she dukkers.
Can she dukker misto?
There's kekkeny Romany juva tuley the can for dukkering
sar Rawnie Wardomescri; nastis not to be dukker'd by lati;
she's a tatchi chovahan; shelels foky by the wast and dukkers
lende, whether they cams or kek.

*Do you know Mrs. Cooper?
I knows her very well, brother.
Do you like her?
I loves her very much, brother; and I have often, often said
to the other Gypsies, when they were speaking ill of her: She's
a gentlewoman; she takes care of all of you; if it were not for
her, you would all go to the devil.
What does she do for a living?
She tells fortunes, brother; she tell fortunes.
Is she a good hand at fortune-telling?
There's no Roman woman under the sun so good at fortune-
telling as Mrs. Cooper; it is impossible not to have your fortune*

told by her; she's a true witch; she takes people by the hand, and tells their fortunes, whether they will or no.

Kek koskipen si to jal roddring after Romany Chals. When tute came to dick lende nestist to latch yeck o' lende; but when tute's penching o' wafor covars tute dicks o' lende dosta dosta.

'Tis no use to go seeking after Gypsies. When you wants to see them 'tis impossible to find one of them; but when you are thinking of other matters you see plenty, plenty of them.

Mande will sollohaul neither bango nor tatcho against kekkeno; if they cams to latch abri chomoni, muk lende latch it abri their cokkoré.

I will swear neither falsely nor truly against any one; if they wishes to find out something, let them find it out themselves.

If he had been bitcheno for a boro luripen mande would have penn'd chi; but it kairs mande diviou to pentch that he was bitcheno, all along of a bori lubbeny, for trin tringurishis ta posh.

If he had been transported for a great robbery, I would have said nothing; but it makes me mad to think that he has been sent away, all along of a vile harlot, for the value of three-and-sixpence.

When he had kair'd the moripen, he kair'd sig and plastrar'd adrey the wesh, where he gared himself drey the hev of a boro, puro rukh; but it was kek koskipen asarlus; the plastra-mengres slomm'd his piré sore along the wesh till they well'd to the rukh.

When he had committed the murder he made haste, and ran into the wood, where he hid himself in the hollow of a great old tree; but it was of no use at all; the runners followed his track all along the forest till they came to the tree.

Sau kisi foky has tute dukker'd to divvus?
Yeck rawnie coccori, prala; dov ody she wels palal; mande
jins lati by the kaulo dori prey laki shubba.
Sau bute luvvu did she del tute?
Yeck gurush, prala; yeck gurush coccoro. The beng te lilly a
truppy!

How many fortunes have you told to-day?
Only one lady's, brother; yonder she's coming back; I knows
her by the black lace on her gown.
How much money did she give you?
One groat, brother; only one groat. May the devil run away
with her bodily!

Shoon the kosko rokkrapen so Micail jinney-mengro penn'd
ke Rawnie Trullifer: Rawnie Trollopr, you must jib by your
jibben: and if a base se tukey you must chiv lis tuley.

Hear the words of wisdom which Mike the Grecian said to
Mrs. Trullifer: Mrs. Trollopr, you must live by your living;
and if you have a pound you must spend it.

Can you rokkra Romanes?
Avali, prala!
So si Weshenjuggalslomomengreskeytemskeytudlogueri?
Mande don't jin what you pens, prala.
Then tute is kek Romano lavomengro.

Can you speak Romany?
Aye, aye, brother!
What is Weshenjuggalslomomengreskeytemskeytudlogueri?
I don't know what you say, brother
Then you are no master of Romany.

Romane Navior of Temes and Gavior

Gypsy Names of Countries and Towns

Baulo-mengreskey tem	Swineherds' country	Hampshire
Bitcheno padlengreskey tem	Transported fellows' country	Botany Bay
Bokra-mengreskey tem	Shepherds' country	Sussex
Bori-congriken gav	Great church town	York
Boro-rukeneskey gav	Great tree town	Fairlop
Boro gueroneskey tem	Big fellows' country	Northumberland
Chohawniskey tem	Witches' country	Lancashire
Choko-mengreskey gav	Shoemakers' town	Northampton
Churi-mengreskey gav	Cutlers' town	Sheffield
Coro-mengreskey tem	Potters' country	Staffordshire
Cosht-killimengreskey tem	Cudgel players' country	Cornwall
Curo-mengreskey gav	Boxers' town	Nottingham
Dinelo tem	Fools' country	Suffolk
Giv-engreskey tem	Farmers' country	Buckinghamshire
Gry-engreskey gav	Horsedealers' town	Horncastle
Guyo-mengreskey tem	Pudding-eaters' country	Yorkshire
Hindity-mengreskey tem	Dirty fellows' country	Ireland
Jinney-mengreskey gav	Sharpers' town	Manchester
Juggal-engreskey gav	Dog-fanciers' town	Dudley
Juvlo-mengreskey tem	Lousy fellows' country	Scotland
Kaulo gav	The black town	Birmingham
Levin-engriskey tem	Hop country	Kent
Lil-engreskey gav	Book fellows' town	Oxford
Match-eneskey gav	Fishy town	Yarmouth
Mi-develeskey gav	My God's town	Canterbury
Mi-krauliskey gav	Royal town	London
Nashi-mescro gav	Racers' town	Newmarket
Pappin-eskey tem	Duck country	Lincolnshire
Paub-pawnugo tem	Apple-water country	Herefordshire

Porrum-engreskey tem	Leek-eaters' country	Wales
Pov-engreskey tem	Potato country	Norfolk
Rashayeskey gav	Clergyman's town	Ely
Rokrengreskey gav	Talking fellows' town	Norwich
Shammin-engreskey gav	Chairmakers' town	Windsor
Tudlo tem	Milk country	Cheshire
Weshen-eskey gav	Forest town	Epping
Weshen-juggal-slommo- mengreskey tem	Fox-hunting fellows' country	Leicestershire
Wongareskey gav	Coal town	Newcastle
Wusto-mengresky tem	Wrestlers' country	Devonshire

Thomas Rossar-Mescro

Prey Juniken bis diuto divvus, drey the besh yeck mille ochto shel shovardesh ta trin, mande jaw'd to dick Thomas Rossar-mescro, a puro Romano, of whom mande had shoon'd bute. He was jibbing drey a tan naveno Rye Groby's Court, kek dur from the Coromengreskoe Tan ta Bokkar-engreskey Wesh. When mande dick'd leste he was beshing prey the poov by his wuddur, chiving misto the poggado tuleskey part of a skammin. His ker was posh ker, posh wardo, and stood drey a corner of the tan; kek dur from lesti were dui or trin wafor ker-wardoes. There was a wafudo canipen of baulor, though mande dick'd kekkeney. I penn'd "Sarshin?" in Romany jib, and we had some rokrapen kettaney. He was a boro mush, as mande could dick, though he was beshing. But though boro he was kek tulo, ta lescré wastes were tarney sar yek rawnie's. Lollo leste mui sar yeck weneskoe paub, ta lescro bal rather lollo than parno. Prey his shero was a beti stadj, and he was kek wafudo riddo. On my putching leste kisi boro he was, ta kisi puro, he penn'd that he was sho piré sore but an inch boro, ta enyovardesh ta dui besh puro. He didn't jin to rokkra bute in Romano, but jinn'd almost sore so mande rokkar'd te leste. Moro rokkrapen was mostly in gorgiko jib. Yeck covar yecklo drey lescro drom of rokkring mande pennsch'd kosko to rig in zi. In tan of penning Romany, sar wafor Romany chals, penn'd o Roumany, a lav which sig, sig rigg'd to my zi *Roumain*, the tatcho, puro nav of the Vallackiskie jib and foky. He seem'd a biti aladge of being of Romany rat. He penn'd that he was beano drey the Givengreskey Tem, that he was kek tatcho Romano, but yeckly posh ta posh: lescro dado was Romano, but lescri daya a gorgie of the Lilengreskoe Gav; he had never camm'd bute to jib

Romaneskoenaes, and when tarno had been a givengreskoe raklo. When he was boro he jall'd adrey the Lilengrotemskey militia, and was desh ta stor besh a militia curomengro. He had jall'd bute about Engli-tem and the juvalo-mengreskey, Tem, drey the cheeros of the puri chingaripen, and had been adrey Monseer-tem, having volunteered to jal odoy to cour agen the parley-woo gueros. He had dick'd Bordeaux and the boro gav Paris. After the chingaripen, he had lell'd oprey skamminengring, and had jall'd about the tem, but had been knau for buter than trianda beshor jibbing in Lundra. He had been romado, but his romadi had been mullee bute, bute cheeros; she had dinn'd leste yeck chavo, so was knau a heftwardesh beshengro, dicking bute puroder than yo cocoro, ta kanau lying naflo of a tatti naflipen drey yeck of the wardes. He penn'd that at yeck cheeros he could kair dosta luvvu by skamminengring, but kanau from his bori puripen could scarcely kair yeck tringurushee a divvus. "Ladjipen si," I penn'd, "that a mush so puro as tute should have to booty." "Kosko zi! kosko zi!" he penn'd; "Paracrow Dibble that mande is dosta ruslo to booty, and that mande has koskey camomescres; I shan't be tugnis to jib to be a shel beshengro, though tatchipen si if mande was a rye mande would kair kek booty." His chaveskoe chavo, a trianda ta pansch beshengro, well'd kanau ta rokkar'd mansar. He was a misto dicking ta rather misto riddo mush, sar chimouni jinneymengreskey drey lescro mui. He penn'd that his dadeskoe dad was a fino puro mush, savo had dick'd bute, and that dosta, dosta foky well'd odoy to shoon lescré rokkrapenes of the puro cheeros, of the Franciskie ta Americanskie chingaripenes, and of what yo had dick'd drey wafu tems. That tatchipen to pen there was a cheeros when his drom was dur from kosko, for that he camm'd to cour, sollohaul ta kair himself motto, but that kanau he was a wafu mush, that he had muk'd sore curopen and wafudo rokkrapen, and, to corauni sore, was yeck tee-totaller, yo cocoro having kair'd leste sollohaul that he would pi kekomi neither tatti panie nor levinor: that he jall'd sore the curques either to congri or Tabernacle, and that tho' he kek jinn'd to del oprey he camm'd to shoon the Miduveleskoe lil dell'd oprey to leste; that the parishkie ryor held leste drey boro camopen, and that the congriskoe rashi, and oprey sore Dr. P. of the Tabernacle had a boro opinionos of leste, ta

penn'd that he would hal the Miduveleskoe habben sar moro
Araunyo Jesus drey the kosko tem opral. Mande putch'd
whether the Romany chals well'd often to dick leste? He
penn'd that they well'd knau and then to pen Koshto divvus
and Sarshin? but dov' odoy was sore; that neither his
dadeskoe dad nor yo cocoro camm'd to dick lende, because
they were wafodu foky, perdo of wafodupen and bango
camopen, ta oprey sore bute envȳous; that drey the wen they
jall'd sore cattaney to the ryor, and rokkar'd wafodu of the
puro mush, and pukker'd the ryor to let lester a coppur which
the ryor had lent leste, to kair tatto his choveno puro truppo
drey the cheeros of the trashlo shillipen; that tatchipen si
their wafodupen kaired the puro mush kek dosh, for the ryor
pukker'd lende to jal their drom and be aladge of their cocoré,
but that it was kek misto to pensch that yeck was of the same
rat as such foky. After some cheeros I dinn'd the puro mush a
tawno cuttor of rupe, shook leste by ye wast, penn'd that it
would be mistos amande to dick leste a shel-beshengro, and
jaw'd away keri.

Thomas Herne

*On the twenty-second day of June, in the year one thousand
eight hundred and sixty-three, I went to see Thomas Herne,
an old Gypsy, of whom I had heard a great deal. He was
living at a place called Mr. Groby's Court, not far from the
Potteries and the Shepherd's Bush. When I saw him, he was
sitting on the ground by his door, mending the broken bottom
of a chair. His house was half-house half-waggon, and stood in
a corner of the court; not far from it were two or three other
waggon-houses. There was a disagreeable smell of hogs, though
I saw none. I said, "How do you do?" in the Gypsy tongue,
and we had some discourse together. He was a tall man, as I
could see, though he was sitting. But, though tall, he was not
stout, and his hands were small as those of a lady. His face*

was as red as a winter apple, and his hair was rather red than grey. He had a small hat on his head, and he was not badly dressed. On my asking him how tall he was, and how old, he said that he was six foot high, all but an inch, and that he was ninety-two years old. He could not talk much Gypsy, but understood almost all that I said to him. Our discourse was chiefly in English. One thing only in his manner of speaking I thought worthy of remembrance. Instead of saying Romany, like other Gypsies, he said Roumany, a word which instantly brought to my mind Roumain, the genuine, ancient name of the Wallachian tongue and people. He seemed to be rather ashamed of being of Gypsy blood. He told me that he was born in Buckinghamshire, that he was no true Gypsy, but only half-and-half: his father was a Gypsy, but his mother was a Gentile of Oxford; he had never had any particular liking for the Gypsy manner of living, and when little had been a farmer's boy. When he grew up he enlisted into the Oxford militia, and was fourteen years a militia soldier. He had gone much about England and Scotland in the time of the old war, and had been in France, having volunteered to go thither to fight against the French. He had seen Bordeaux and the great city of Paris. After the war he had taken up chair-making, and had travelled about the country, but had been now for more than thirty years living in London. He had been married, but his wife had long been dead. She had borne him a son, who was now a man seventy years of age, looking much older than himself, and at present lying sick of a burning fever in one of the caravans. He said that at one time he could make a good deal of money by chair-making, but now from his great age could scarcely earn a shilling a day. "What a shame," said I, "that a man so old as you should have to work at all!" "Courage! courage!" he cried; "I thank God that I am strong enough to work, and that I have good friends; I shan't be sorry to live to be a hundred years old, though true it is that if I were a gentleman I would do no work." His grandson, a man of about five-and-thirty, came now and conversed with me. He was a good-looking and rather well-dressed man, with something of a knowing card in his countenance. He said that his grandfather was a fine old man, who had seen a great deal, and that a great many people came to hear his stories of the old time, of the French and American wars, and of what *he had seen in other countries. That, truth to say, there was a time when his way was far from commendable, for that he loved to fight, swear, and make himself drunk; but that now he was another man, that he had abandoned all fighting and evil speaking, and, to crown all, was a teetotaller, he himself having made him swear that he would no more drink either gin or ale: that he went every Sunday either to church or Tabernacle, and that, though he did not know how to read, he loved to hear the holy book read to him; that the gentlemen of the parish entertained a great regard for him, and that the church clergyman and, above all, Dr. P. of the Tabernacle had a high opinion of him, and said that he would partake of the holy banquet with our Lord Jesus in the blessed country above. On my inquiring whether the Gypsies came often to see him, he said that they came now and then to say "Good day" and "How do you do?" but that was all; that neither his grandfather nor himself cared to see them, because they were evil people, full of wickedness and left-handed love, and, above all, very envyous; that in the winter they all went in a body to the gentlemen and spoke ill of the old man, and begged the gentlemen to take from him a blanket which the gentlemen had lent him to warm his poor old body with in the time of the terrible cold; that it is true their wickedness did the old man no harm, for the gentlemen told them to go away and be ashamed of themselves, but that it was not pleasant to think that one was of the same blood as such people. After some time I gave the old man a small piece of silver, shook him by the hand, said that I should be glad to see him live to be a hundred, and went away home.*

Kokkodus Artarus

Drey the puro cheeros there jibb'd a puri Romani juva, Sinfaya laki nav. Tatchi Romani juva i; caum'd to rokkra Romany, nav'd every mush kokkodus, ta every mushi deya. Yeck chavo was láki; lescro nav Artáros; dinnelo or diviou was O; romadi was lesgué; but the rommadi merr'd, mukking leste yeck chávo. Artáros caum'd to jal oprey the drom, and sikker his nangipen to rawnies and kair muior. At last the ryor chiv'd leste drey the diviou ker. The chávo jibb'd with his puri deya till he was a desch ta pantsch besh engro. Yeck divvus a Romani juva jalling along the drom dick'd the puri juva beshing tuley a bor roving: What's the matter, Sinfaya, pukker'd i?

My chavo's chavo is lell'd oprey, deya.
What's he lell'd oprey for?
For a meila and posh, deya.
Why don't you jal to dick leste?
I have nash'd my maila, deya.
O má be tugni about your maila; jal and dick leste.

I don't jin kah se, deya! diviou kokkodus Artáros jins, kek mande. Ah diviou, diviou, jal amande callico.

Mang, Prala

Romano chavo was manging sar bori gudli yeck rye te del les pasherro. Lescri deya so was beshing kek dur from odoy penn'd in gorgikey rokrapen: Meklis juggal, ta av acoi! ma kair the rye kinyo with your gudli! and then penn'd sig in Romany jib: Mang, Prala, mang! Ta o chavo kair'd ajaw till the rye chiv'd les yeck shohaury.

[Something like the following little anecdote is related by the Gypsies in every part of Continental Europe.]

Beg On, Brother

A Gypsy brat was once pestering a gentleman to give him a halfpenny. The mother, who was sitting nigh, cried in English: Leave off, you dog, and come here! don't trouble the gentleman with your noise; and then added in Romany: Beg on, brother! and so the brat did, till the gentleman flung him a sixpence.

English Gypsy Songs

WELLING KATTANEY

Coin si deya, coin se dado?
Pukker mande drey Romanes,
Ta mande pukkeravava tute.

Rossar-mescri minri deya!
Vardo-mescro minro dado!
Coin se dado, coin si deya?
Mande's pukker'd tute drey Romanes;
Knau pukker tute mande.

Petuiengro minro dado!
Purana minri deya!
Tatchey Romany si men —
Mande's pukker'd tute drey Romanes,
Ta tute's pukker'd mande.

THE GYPSY MEETING

Who's your mother, who's your father?
Do thou answer me in Romany,
And I will answer thee.

A Hearne I have for mother!
A Cooper for my father!
Who's your father, who's your mother?
I have answer'd thee in Romany,
Now do thou answer me.

A Smith I have for father!
A Lee I have for mother!
True Romans both are we —
For I've answer'd thee in Romany,
And thou hast answer'd me.

"Av, my little Romany chei!
  Av along with mansar!
Av, my little Romany chel!
  Koshto si for mangue."

"I shall lel a curapen,
  If I jal aley;
I shall lel a curapen
  From my dear bebee."

"I will jal on my chongor,
  Then I'll pootch your bebee.
'O my dear bebee, dey me your chi,
  For koshto si for mangue.'

"'Since you pootch me for my chi,
  I will dey you lati.'"
Av, my little Romany chel!
  We will jal to the wafu tem:

"I will chore a beti gry,
  And so we shall lel cappi."
"Kekko, meero mushipen,
  For so you would be stardo;

"But I will jal a dukkering,
  And so we shall lel cappi."
"Koshto, my little Romany chel!
  Koshto si for mangue."

MAKING A FORTUNE

*"Come along, my little gypsy girl,
  Come along, my little dear;
Come along, my little gypsy girl —
  We'll wander far and near."*

*"I should get a leathering
  Should I with thee go;
I should get a leathering
  From my dear aunt, I trow."*

"*I'll go down on my two knees,*
  And I will beg your aunt.
'O auntie dear, give me your child;
  She's just the girl I want!'

"'*Since you ask me for my child,*
  I will not say thee no!'
Come along, my little gypsy girl!
  To another land we'll go:

"*I will steal a little horse,*
  And our fortunes make thereby."
"*Not so, my little gypsy boy,*
  For then you'd swing on high;

"*But I'll a fortune-telling go,*
  And our fortunes make thereby."
"*Well said, my little gypsy girl,*
  You counsel famously."

LELLING CAPPI

No. 2

"Av, my little Rumni chel,
  Av along with mansar;
We will jal a gry-choring
  Pawdle across the chumba.

"I'll jaw tuley on my chongor
  To your deya and your bebee;
And I'll pootch lende that they del
  Tute to me for romadi."

"I'll jaw with thee, my Runni chal,
  If my dye and bebee muk me;
But choring gristurs traishes me,
  For it brings one to the rukie.

"'Twere ferreder that you should ker,
  Petuls and I should dukker,
For then adrey our tarney tan,
  We kek atraish may sova."

"Kusko, my little Rumni chel,
    Your rokrapen is kusko;
We'll dukker and we'll petuls ker
    Pawdle across the chumba.

"O kusko si to chore a gry
    Adrey the kaulo rarde;
But 'tis not kosko to be nash'd
    Oprey the nashing rukie."

MAKING A FORTUNE

No. 2

"Come along, my little gypsy girl,
    Come along with me, I pray!
A-stealing horses we will go,
    O'er the hills so far away.

"Before your mother and your aunt
    I'll down upon my knee,
And beg they'll give me their little girl
    To be my Romadie."

"I'll go with you, my gypsy boy,
    If my mother and aunt agree;
But a perilous thing is horse-stealinge,
    For it brings one to the tree.

"'Twere better you should tinkering ply,
    And I should fortunes tell;
For then within our little tent
    In safety we might dwell."

"Well said, my little gypsy girl,
    I like well what you say;
We'll tinkering ply, and fortunes tell
    O'er the hills so far away.

"'Tis a pleasant thing in a dusky night
    A horse-stealing to go;
But to swing in the wind on the gallows-tree,
    Is no pleasant thing, I trow."

THE DUI CHALOR

Dui Romany Chals were bitcheney,
Bitcheney pawdle the bori pawnee.
Plato for kawring,
Lasho for choring
The putsi of a bori rawnee.

And when they well'd to the wafu tem,
The tem that's pawdle the bori pawnee,
Plato was nasho
Sig, but Lasho
Was lell'd for rom by a bori rawnee.

You cam to jin who that rawnie was,
'Twas the rawnie from whom he chor'd the putsee:
The Chal had a black
Chohauniskie yack,
And she slomm'd him pawdle the bori pawnee.

THE TWO GYPSIES

Two Gypsy lads were transported,
Were sent across the great water.
Plato was sent for rioting,
And Louis for stealing the purse
Of a great lady.

And when they came to the other country,
The country that lies across the great water,
Plato was speedily hung,
But Louis was taken as a husband
By a great lady.

You wish to know who was the lady,
'Twas the lady from whom he stole the purse:
The Gypsy had a black and witching eye,
And on account of that she followed him
Across the great water.

MIRO ROMANY CHI

As I was a jawing to the gav yeck divvus
I met on the drom miro Romany chi;
I pootch'd las whether she come sar mande,
And she penn'd tu sar wafo rommadis;
O mande there is kek wafo romady,
So penn'd I to miro Romany chi,
And I'll kair tute miro tatcho romadi
If you but pen tu come sar mande.

MY ROMAN LASS

As I to the town was going one day
My Roman lass I met by the way;
Said I: Young maid, will you share my lot?
Said she: Another wife you've got.
Ah no! to my Roman lass I cried;
No wife have I in the world so wide,
And you my wedded wife shall be
If you will consent to come with me.

AVA, CHI

Hokka tute mande
Mande pukkra bebee
Mande shauvo tute —
Ava, Chi!

YES, MY GIRL

If to me you prove untrue,
Quickly I'll your auntie tell
I've been over-thick with you —
Yes, my girl, I will.

THE TEMESKOE RYE

Penn'd the temeskoe rye to the Romany chi,
As the choon was dicking prey lende dui:
Rinkeny tawni, Romany rawni,
Mook man choom teero gudlo mui.

THE YOUTHFUL EARL

Said the youthful earl to the Gypsy girl,
As the moon was casting its silver shine:
Brown little lady, Egyptian lady,
Let me kiss those sweet lips of thine.

CAMO-GILLIE

Pawnie birks
My men-engri shall be;
Yackors my dudes
Like ruppeney shine:
Atch meery chi!
Mā jal away:
Perhaps I may not dick tute
Kek komi.

LOVE-SONG

I'd choose as pillows for my head
Those snow-white breasts of thine;
I'd use as lamps to light my bed
Those eyes of silver shine:
O lovely maid, disdain me not,
Nor leave me in my pain:
Perhaps 'twill never be my lot
To see thy face again.

TUGNIS AMANDE

I'm jalling across the pāni —
A choring mas and morro,
Along with a bori lubbeny,
And she has been the ruin of me.

I sov'd yeck rarde drey a gran,
A choring mas and morro,
Along with a bori lubbeny,
And she has been the ruin of me.

She pootch'd me on the collico,
A choring mass and morro,
To jaw with lasa to the show,
For she would be the ruin of me.

And when I jaw'd odoy with lasa,
A choring mas and morro,
Sig she chor'd a rawnie's kissi,
And so she was the ruin of me.

They lell'd up lata, they lell'd up mande,
A choring mas and morro,
And bitch'd us dui pawdle pāni,
So she has been the ruin of me.

I'm jalling across the pāni,
A choring mas and morro,
Along with a bori lubbeny,
And she has been the ruin of me.

WOE IS ME

I'm sailing across the water,
A-stealing bread and meat so free,
Along with a precious harlot,
And she has been the ruin of me.

I slept one night within a barn,
A-stealing bread and meat so free,
Along with a precious harlot,
And she has been the ruin of me.

Next morning she would have me go,
A-stealing bread and meat so free,
To see with her the wild-beast show,
For she would be the ruin of me.

I went with her to see the show,
A-stealing bread and meat so free,
To steal a purse she was not slow,
And so she was the ruin of me.

They took us up, and with her I,
A-stealing bread and meat so free:
Am sailing now to Botany,
So she has been the ruin of me.

I'm sailing across the water,
A-stealing bread and meat so free,
Along with a precious harlot,
And she has been the ruin of me.

THE RYE AND RAWNIE

The rye he mores adrey the wesh
   The kaun-engro and chiriclo;
You sovs with leste drey the wesh,
   And rigs for leste the gono.

Oprey the rukh adrey the wesh
   Are chiriclo and chiricli;
Tuley the rukh adrey the wesh
   Are pireno and pireni.

THE SQUIRE AND LADY

The squire he roams the good greenwood,
   And shoots the pheasant and the hare;
Thou sleep'st with him in good green wood,
   And dost for him the game-sack bear.

I see, I see upon the tree
   The little male and female dove;
Below the tree I see, I see
   The lover and his lady love.

ROMANY SUTTUR GILLIE

Jaw to sutturs, my tiny chal;
Your die to dukker has jall'd abri;
At rarde she will wel palal
And tute of her tud shall pie.

Jaw to lutherum, tiny baw!
I'm teerie deya's purie mam;
As tute cams her tud canaw
Thy deya meerie tud did cam.

GYPSY LULLABY

Sleep thee, little tawny boy!
  Thy mother's gone abroad to spae,
Her kindly milk thou shalt enjoy
  When home she comes at close of day.

Sleep thee, little tawny guest!
  Thy mother is my daughter fine;
As thou dost love her kindly breast,
  She once did love this breast of mine.

SHARRAFI KRALYISSA

Finor coachey innar Lundra,
Bonor coachey innar Lundra,
Finor coachey, bonor coachey
Mande dick'd innar Lundra.

Bonor, finor coachey
Mande dick'd innar Lundra
The divvus the Kralyissa jall'd
To congri innar Lundra.

OUR BLESSED QUEEN

Coaches fine in London,
Coaches good in London,
Coaches fine and coaches good
I did see in London.

Coaches good and coaches fine
I did see in London,
The blessed day our blessed Queen
Rode to church in London.

PLASTRA LESTI!

Gare yourselves, pralor!
Mā pee kek-komi!
The guero's welling —
Plastra lesti!

RUN FOR IT

Up, up, brothers!
  Cease your revels!
The Gentile's coming —
  Run like devils!

Foreign Gypsy Songs

Oy die-la, oy mama-la oy!
Cherie podey mangue penouri.

Russian Gypsy Song.

THE ROMANY SONGSTRESS

From the Russian Gypsy

Her temples they are aching,
As if wine she had been taking;
Her tears are every springing,
Abandoned is her singing!
She can neither eat nor rest
With love she's so distress'd;
At length she's heard to say:
"Oh here I cannot stay,
Go saddle me my steed,
To my lord I must proceed;
In his palace plenteously
Both eat and drink shall I;
The servants far and wide,
Bidding guests shall run and ride.
And when within the hall the multitude I see,
I'll raise my voice anew, and sing in Romany."

L'ERAJAI

Un erajai
Sinaba chibando un sermon;
Y lle falta un balicho
Al chindomar de aquel gao,
Y lo chanelaba que los Cales
Lo abian nicabao;
Y penela l'erajai, "Chaboró!
Guillate a tu quer
Y nicabela la perí
Que terela el balicho,
Y chibela andro
Una lima de tun chaborí,
Chabori,
Una lima de tun chaborí."

THE FRIAR

From the Spanish Gypsy

A Friar
Was preaching once with zeal and with fire;
And a butcher of the town
Had lost a flitch of bacon;
And well the friar knew
That the Gypsies it had taken;
So suddenly he shouted: "Gypsy, ho!
Hie home, and from the pot
Take the flitch of bacon out,
The flitch good and fat,
And in its place throw
A clout, a dingy clout of thy brat,
Of thy brat,
A clout, a dingy clout of thy brat."

Chaló Malbrun chingarár,
Birandón, birandón, birandéra!
Chaló Malbrun chingarár;
No sé bus truterá!
No sé bus truterá!

La romi que le caméla,
Birandón, birandón, birandéra!
La romi que le camela
Muy curepeñada está,
Muy curepeñada está.

S'ardéla á la felichá,
Birandón, birandón, birandéra!
S'ardéla á la felichá
Y baribu dur dicá,
Y baribu dur dicá.

Dicá abillar su burno,
Birandón, birandón, birandéra!
Dicá abillar su burno,
En ropa callardá,
En ropa callardá.

"Burno, lacho quirbó;
Birandón, birandón, birandéra!
Burno, lacho quiribó,
Que nuevas has diñar?
Que nuevas has diñar?"

"Las nuevas que io térelo,
Birandón, birandón, birandéra!
Las nuevas que io terélo
Te haran orobar,
Te haran orobar.

"Meró Malbrun mi eráy,
Birandón, birandón, birandéra!
Meró Malbrun mi eráy
Meró en la chingá,
Meró en la chingá.

"Sinaba á su entierro,
Birandón, birandón, birandéra!
Sinaba á su entierro
La plastani sará,
La plastani sará.

"Seis guapos jundunáres,
Birandón, birandón, birandéra!
Seis guapos jundunáres
Le lleváron cabañar,
Le lleváron cabañar.

"Delante de la jestári,
Birandón, birandón, birandéra!
Delante de la jestári
Chaló el sacristá,
Chaló el sacristá.

"El sacristá delante,
Birandón, birandón, birandéra!
El sacristá delante,
Y el errajai palá,
Y el errajai palá.

"Al majaro ortaláme,
Birandón, birandón, birandéra!
Al majaro ortaláme
Le lleváron cabañar,
Le lleváron cabañar.

"Y oté le cabañáron
Birandón, birandón, birandéra!
Y oté le cabañáron
No dur de la burdá,
No dur de la burdá.

"Y opré de la jestári
Birandón, birandón, birandéra!
Guillabéla un chilindróte;
Sobá en paz, sobá!
Sobá en paz, sobá!

From the Spanish Gypsy Version

Malbrouk is gone to the wars,
Birrandón, birrandón, birrandéra!
Malbrouk is gone to the wars;
He'll never return no more!
He'll never return no more!

His lady-love and darling,
Birrandón, birrandón, birrandéra!
His lady-love and darling
His absence doth deplore,
His absence doth deplore.

To the turret's top she mounted,
Birrandón, birrandón, birrandéra!
To the turret's top she mounted
And look'd till her eyes were sore,
And look'd till her eyes were sore.

She saw his squire a-coming,
Birrandón, birrandón, birrandéra!
She saw his squire a-coming;
And a mourning suit he wore,
And a mourning suit he wore.

"O squire, my trusty fellow;
Birrandón, birrandón, birrandéra!
O squire, my trusty fellow,
What news of my soldier poor?
What news of my soldier poor?"

"The news which I bring thee, lady,
Birrandón, birrandón, birrandéra!
The news which I bring thee, lady,
Will cause thy tears to shower,
Will cause thy tears to shower.

"Malbrouk my master's fallen,
Birrandón, birrandón, birrandéra!
Malbrouk my master's fallen,
He fell on the fields of gore,
He fell on the fields of gore.

"His funeral attended,
Birrandón, birrandón, birrandéra!
His funeral attended
The whole reg'mental corps,
The whole reg'mental corps.

"Six neat and proper soldiers,
Birrandón, birrandón, birrandéra!
Six neat and proper soldiers
To the grave my master bore,
To the grave my master bore.

"The parson follow'd the coffin,
Birrandón, birrandón, birrandéra!
The parson follow'd the coffin,
And the sexton walk'd before,
And the sexton walk'd before.

"They buried him in the churchyard,
Birrandón, birrandón, birrandéra!
They buried him in the churchyard,
Not far from the church's door,
Not far from the church's door.

"And there above his coffin,
Birrandón, birrandón, birrandéra!
There sings a little swallow:
Sleep there, thy toils are o'er,
Sleep there, thy toils are o'er."

The English Gypsies

TUGNEY BESHOR

The Romany chals
Should jin so bute
As the Puro Beng
To scape of gueros
And wafo gorgies
The wafodupen.

They lels our gryor,
They lels our wardoes,
And wusts us then
Drey starripenes
To mer of pishens
And buklipen.

Cauna volélan
Muley pappins
Pawdle the len
Men artavàvam
Of gorgio foky
The wafodupen.
      Ley teero sollohanloinus opreylis!

SORROWFUL YEARS

The wit and the skill
Of the Father of ill,
Who's clever indeed,
If they would hope
With their foes to cope
The Romany need.

Our horses they take,
Our waggons they break,
And us they fling
Into horrid cells,
Where hunger dwells
And vermin sting.

When the dead swallow
The fly shall follow
Across the river,
O we'll forget
The wrongs we've met,
But till then O never:
    Brother, of that be certain.

The English Gypsies call themselves Romany Chals and Romany Chies, that is, Sons and Daughters of Rome. When speaking to each other, they say "Pal" and "Pen"; that is, brother and sister. All people not of their own blood they call "Gorgios," or Gentiles. Gypsies first made their appearance in England about the year 1480. They probably came from France, where tribes of the race had long been wandering about under the names of Bohemians and Egyptians. In England they pursued the same kind of merripen* which they and their ancestors had pursued on the Continent. They roamed about in bands, consisting of thirty, sixty, or ninety families, with light, creaking carts, drawn by horses and donkeys, encamping at night in the spots they deemd convenient. The women told fortunes at the castle of the baron and the cottage of the yeoman; filched gold and silver coins from the counters of money-changers; caused the death of hogs in farmyards, by means of a stuff called drab or drao, which affects the brain, but does not corrupt the blood; and subsequently begged, and generally obtained, the carcases. The men plied tinkering and brasiery, now and then stole horses, and occasionally ventured upon highway robbery.

---

* "Merripen" means life, and likewise death; even as "collico" means tomorrow as well as yesterday, and perhaps "sorlo," evening as well as morning.

The writer has here placed the Chies before the Chals, because as he frequently had occasion to observe, the Gypsy women are by far more remarkable beings than the men. It is the Chi and not the Chal who has caused the name of Gypsy to be a sound awaking wonder, awe, and curiosity in every part of the civilised world. Not that there have never been remarkable men of the Gypsy race both abroad and at home. Duke Michael, as he was called, the leader of the great Gypsy horde which suddenly made its appearance in Germany at the beginning of the fifteenth century, was no doubt a remarkable man; the Gitano Conde, whom Martin del Rio met at Toledo a hundred years afterwards, who seemed to speak all languages, and to be perfectly acquainted with the politics of all the Courts of Europe, must certainly have been a remarkable man; so, no doubt, here at home was Boswell; so undoubtedly was Cooper, called by the gentlemen of the Fives Court — poor fellows! they are all gone now — the "wonderful little Gypsy"; — but upon the whole the poetry, the sorcery, the devilry, if you please to call it so, are vastly on the side of the women. How blank and inanimate is the countenance of the Gypsy man, even when trying to pass off a foundered donkey as a flying dromedary, in comparison with that of the female Romany, peering over the wall of a par-yard at a jolly hog!

Shar shin Sinfye?
Koshto divvus, Romany Chi!
So shan tute kairing acoi?

Sinfye, Sinfye! how do you do?
Daughter of Rome, good day to you!
What are you thinking here to do?

After a time the evil practices of the Gypsies began to be noised about, and terrible laws were enacted against people "using the manner of Egyptians" — Chies were scourged by dozens, Chals hung by scores. Throughout the reign of Elizabeth there was a terrible persecution of the Gypsy race; far less, however, on account of the crimes which they actually committed, than from a suspicion which was entertained that they harboured amidst their companies priests and emissaries of Rome, who had come to England for the purpose of sowing sedition and inducing the people to embrace again the old discarded superstition. This suspicion, however, was entirely without foundation. The Gypsies call each other brother and sister, and are not in the habit of admitting to their fellowship people of a different blood and with whom they have no sympathy. There was, however, a description of wandering people at that time, even as there is at present, with whom the priests, who are described as going about, sometimes disguised as serving-men, sometimes as broken soldiers, sometimes as shipwrecked mariners, would experience no difficulty in associating, and with whom, in all probability, they occasionally did associate — the people called in Acts of Parliament sturdy beggars and vagrants, in the old cant language Abraham men, and in the modern Pikers. These people have frequently been confounded with the Gypsies, but are in reality a distinct race, though they resemble the latter in some points. They roam about like the Gypsies, and, like them, have a kind of secret language. But the Gypsies are a people of Oriental origin, whilst the Abrahamites are the scurf of the English body corporate. The language of the Gypsies is a real language, more like the Sanscrit than any other language in the world; whereas the speech of the Abrahamites is a horrid jargon, composed for the most part of low English words used in an allegorical sense — a jargon in which a stick is called a crack; a hostess, a rum necklace; a bar-maid, a dolly-mort; brandy, rum booze; a constable, a horny. But enough of these Pikers, these Abrahamites. Sufficient to observe that if the disguised priests associated with wandering companies it must have been with these people, who admit anybody to their society, and not with the highly exclusive race the Gypsies.

For nearly a century and a half after the death of Elizabeth the Gypsies seem to have been left tolerably to themselves, for the laws are almost silent respecting them. Chies, no doubt, were occasionally scourged for cauring, that is filching gold and silver coins, and Chals hung for gry-choring, that is horse-stealing; but those are little incidents not much regarded in Gypsy merripen. They probably lived a life during the above period tolerably satisfactory to themselves

— they are not an ambitious people, and there is no word for glory in their language — but next to nothing is known respecting them. A people called Gypsies are mentioned, and to a certain extent treated of, in two remarkable works — one a production of the seventeenth, the other of the eighteenth century — the first entitled the 'English Rogue, or the Adventures of Merriton Latroon,' the other the 'Life of Bamfield Moore Carew'; but those works, though clever and entertaining, and written in the raciest English, are to those who seek for information respecting Gypsies entirely valueless, the writers having evidently mistaken for Gypsies the Pikers or Abrahamites, as the vocabularies appended to the histories, and which are professedly vocabularies of the Gypsy language, are nothing of the kind, but collections of words and phrases belonging to the Abrahamite or Piker jargon. At the commencement of the last century, and for a considerable time afterwards, there was a loud cry raised against the Gypsy women for stealing children. This cry, however, was quite as devoid of reason as the suspicion entertained of old against the Gypsy communities of harbouring disguised priests. Gypsy women, as the writer had occasion to remark many a long year ago, have plenty of children of their own, and have no wish to encumber themselves with those of other people. A yet more extraordinary charge was, likewise, brought against them — that of running away with wenches. Now, the idea of Gypsy women running away with wenches! Where were they to stow them in the event of running away with them? and what were they to do with them in the event of being able to stow them? Nevertheless, two Gypsy women were burnt in the hand in the most cruel and frightful manner, somewhat about the middle of the last century, and two Gypsy men, their relations, sentenced to be hanged, for running away with a certain horrible wench of the name of Elizabeth Canning, who, to get rid of a disgraceful burden, had left her service and gone into concealment for a month, and on her return, in order to account for her absence, said that she had been run away with by Gypsies. The men, however, did not undergo their sentence; for, ere the day appointed for their execution arrived, suspicions beginning to be entertained with respect to the truth of the wench's story, they were reprieved, and, after a little time, the atrocious creature, who had charged people with doing what they neither did nor dreamt of doing, was tried for perjury, convicted, and sentenced to transportation. Yet so great is English infatuation that this Canning, this Elizabeth, had a host of friends, who stood by her, and swore by her to the last, and almost freighted the ship which carried her away with goods, the sale of which enabled her to purchase her freedom of the planter to whom she was consigned, to establish herself in business, and to live in comfort, and almost in luxury, in the New World during the remainder of her life.

But though Gypsies have occasionally experienced injustice; though Patricos and Sherengroes were hanged by dozens in Elizabeth's time on suspicion of harbouring disguised priests; though Gypsy women in the time of the Second George, accused of running away with wenches, were scorched and branded, there can be no doubt that they live in almost continual violation of the laws intended for the protection of society; and it may be added, that in this illegal way of life the women have invariably played a more important part than the men. Of them, amongst other things, it may be said that they are the most accomplished swindlers in the world, their principal victims being people of their own sex, on whose credulity and superstition they practise. Mary Caumlo, or Lovel, was convicted a few years ago at Cardiff of having swindled a surgeon's wife of eighty pounds, under pretence of propitiating certain planets by showing them the money. Not a penny of the booty was ever recovered by the deluded victim; and the Caumli, on leaving the dock, after receiving sentence of a year's imprisonment, turned round and winked to some *brother* or *sister* in court, as mush as to say: *"Mande has gared the luvvu; mande is kek atugni for the besh's starripen"* — "I have hid the money, and care nothing for the year's imprisonment." Young Rawnie P. of N., the daughter of old Rawnie P., suddenly disappeared with the whole capital of an aged and bedridden gentlewoman, amounting to nearly three hundred pounds, whom she had assured that if she were intrusted with it for a short time she should be able to gather certain herbs, from which she could make decoctions, which would restore to the afflicted gentlewoman all her youthful vigour. Mrs. Townsley of the Border was some time ago in trouble at Wick, only twenty-five miles distant from Johnny Groat's House, on a charge of fraudulently obtaining from a fisherman's wife one shilling, two half-crowns, and a five-pound note by promising to untie certain witch-locks, which she had induced her to believe were entwined in the meshes of the fisherman's net, and would, if suffered to remain, prevent him from catching a single herring in the Firth. These events occurred within the last few years, and are sufficiently notorious. They form a triad out of dozens of a similar kind, in some of which there are features so odd, so strangely droll, that indignation against the offence is dispelled by an irresistible desire to laugh.

But Gypsyism is declining, and its days are numbered. There is a force abroad which is doomed to destroy it, a force which never sleepeth either by day or night, and which will not allow the Roman people rest for the soles of their feet. That force is the Rural Police, which, had it been established at the commencement instead of towards the middle of the present century, would have put down Gypsyism long ago. But, recent as its establishment has been, observe what it has produced. Walk from London to Carlisle, but neither by the road's side, nor on heath or common, will you see a single Gypsy tent. True Gypsyism consists in wandering about, in preying upon the Gentiles, but not living amongst them. But such a life is impossible in these days; the Rural Force will not permit it. "It is a hard thing, brother," said old Agamemnon Caumlo to the writer, several years ago; "it is a hard thing, after one has pitched one's little tent, lighted one's little fire, and hung one's kettle by the kettle-iron over it to boil, to have an inspector or constable come up, and say, 'What are you doing here? Take yourself off, you Gypsy dog!' " A hard thing, indeed, old Agamemnon; but there is no help for it. You must e'en live amongst the Gorgios. And for years past the Gypsies have lived amongst the Gorgios, and what has been the result? They do not seem to have improved the Gentiles, and have certainly not been improved by them. By living amongst the Gentiles they have, to a certain extent, lost the only two virtues they possessed. Whilst they lived apart on heaths and commons, and in shadowy lanes, the Gypsy women were paragons of chastity, and the men, if not exactly patterns of sobriety, were, upon the whole, very sober fellows. Such terms, however, are by no means applicable to them at the present day. Sects and castes, even of thieves and murderers, can exist as long as they have certain virtues, which give them a kind of respect in their own eyes; but, losing those virtues, they soon become extinct. When the salt loses its savour, what becomes of it? The Gypsy salt has not altogether lost its savour, but that essential quality is every day becoming fainter, so that there is every reason to suppose that within a few years the English Gypsy caste will have disappeared, merged in the dregs of the English population.

Gypsy Names

There are many curious things connected with the Gypsies, but perhaps nothing more so than what pertains to their names. They have a double nomenclature, each tribe or family having a public and a private name, one by which they are known to the Gentiles, and another to themselves alone. Their public names are quite English; their private ones attempts, some of them highly singular and uncouth, to render those names by Gypsy equivalents. Gypsy names may be divided into two classes, names connected with trades, and surnames or family names. First of all, something about trade names.

There are only two names of trades which have been adopted by English Gypsies as proper names, Cooper and Smith: these names are expressed in the English Gypsy dialect by *Vardo-mescro* and *Petulengro*. The first of these renderings is by no means a satisfactory one, as *Vardo-mescro* means a cartwright, or rather a carter. To speak the truth, it would be next to impossible to render the word 'cooper' into English Gypsy, or indeed into Gypsy of any kind; a cooper, according to the common acceptation of the word, is one who makes pails, tubs, and barrels, but there are no words in Gypsy for such vessels. The Transylvanian Gypsies call a cooper a *bedra-kero* or pail-maker, but *bedra* is not Gypsy, but Hungarian, and the English Gypsies might with equal propriety call a cooper a *pail-engro*. On the whole the English Gypsies did their best when they rendered 'cooper' into their language by the word for 'cartwright.'

Petulengro, the other trade name, is borne by the Gypsies who are known to the public by the English appellation of Smith. It is not very easy to say what is the exact meaning of

Petulengro; it must signify, however, either horseshoe-fellow or tinker: *petali* or *petala* signifies in Gypsy a horseshoe, and is probably derived from the Modern Greek πέταλον; *engro* is an affix, and is either derived from or connected with the Sanscrit *kara*, to make, so that with great feasibility *Petulengro* may be translated horseshoe-maker. But *bedel* in Hebrew means 'tin,' and as there is little more difference between *petul* and *bedel* than between *petul* and *petalon, Petulengro* may be translated with almost equal feasibility by tinker or tin-worker, more especially as tinkering is a principal pursuit of Gypsies, and to *jal petulengring* signifies to go a-tinkering in English Gypsy. Taken, however, in either sense, whether as horseshoe-maker or tin-worker (and, as has been already observed, it must mean one or the other), *Petulengro* may be considered as a tolerably fair rendering of the English Smith.

So much for the names of the Gypsies which the writer has ventured to call trade names; now for those of the other class. These are English surnames, and for the most part of a highly aristocratic character, and it seems at first surprising that people so poor and despised as Gypsies should be found bearing names so time-honoured and imposing. There is, however, a tolerable explanation of the matter in the supposition that on their first arrival in England the different tribes sought the protection of certain grand powerful families, and were permitted by them to locate themselves on their heaths and amid their woodlands, and that they eventually adopted the names of their patrons. Here follow the English names of some of the principal tribes, with the Romany translations or equivalents: —

BOSWELL. — The proper meaning of this word is the town of Bui. The initial *Bo* or *Bui* is an old Northern name, signifying a colonist or settler, one who tills and builds. It was the name of a great many celebrated Northern *kempions*, who won land and a home by hard blows. The last syllable, *well*, is the French *ville*: Boswell, Boston, and Busby all signify one and the same thing — the town of Bui — the *well* being French, the *ton* Saxon, and the *by* Danish; they are half-brothers of Bovil and Belville, both signifying fair town, and which ought to be written Beauville and Belville. The Gypsies, who know and care nothing about etymologies, confounding *bos* with *buss*, a vulgar English verb not to be found in dictionaries, which signifies to kiss, rendered the name Boswell by *Chumomisto*, that is Kisswell, or one who kisses well — *choom* in their language signifying to kiss, and *misto* well — likewise by *choomomescro*, a kisser. Vulgar as the word *buss* may sound at present, it is by no means of vulgar origin, being connected with the Latin *basio* and the Persian *bousè*.

GREY. — This is the name of a family celebrated in English history. The Gypsies who adopted it, rendered it into their language by *Gry*, a word very much resembling it in sound, though not in sense, for *gry*, which is allied to the Sanscrit *ghora*, signifies a horse. They had no better choice, however, for in Romany there is no word for grey, any more than there is for green or blue. In several languages there is a difficulty in expressing the colour which in English is called grey. In Celtic, for instance, there is no definite word for it; *glas*, it is true, is used to express it, but *glas* is as frequently used to express green as it is to express grey.

HEARNE, HERNE. — This is the name of a family which bears the heron for its crest, the name being either derived from the crest, or the crest from the name. There are two Gypsy renderings of the word — *Rossar-mescro* or *Ratzie-mescro*, and *Balor-engre*. *Rossar-mescro* signifies duck-fellow, the duck being substituted for the heron, for which there is no word in Romany. The meaning of *Balor-engre* is hairy people; the translator or translators seeming to have confounded Hearne with 'haaren,' old English for hairs. The latter rendering has never been much in use.

LEE. — The Gypsy name of this tribe is *Purrum*, sometimes pronounced *Purrun*. The meaning of *Purrum* is an onion, and it may be asked what connection can there be between Lee and onion? None whatever: but there is some resemblance in sound between Lee and leek, and it is probable that the Gypsies thought so, and on that account rendered the name by *Purrum*, which, if not exactly a leek, at any rate signifies something which is cousin-german to a leek. It must be borne in mind that in some parts of England the name Lee is spelt Legh and Leigh, which would hardly be the case if at one time it had not terminated in something like a guttural, so that when the Gypsies rendered the name, perhaps nearly four hundred years ago, it sounded very much like 'leek,' and perhaps was Leek, a name derived from the family crest. At first the writer was of opinion that the name was *Purrun*, a modification of *pooro*, which in the Gypsy language signifies old, but speedily came to the conclusion that it must be *Purrum*, a leek or onion; for what possible reason could the Gypsies have for rendering Lee by a word which signifies old or ancient? whereas by rendering it by *Purrum*, they gave themselves a Gypsy name, which, if it did not signify Lee, must to their untutored minds have seemed a very good substitute for Lee. The Gypsy word *pooro*, old, belongs to Hindostan, and is connected with the Sanscrit *pura*, which signifies the same. *Purrum* is a modification of the Wallachian *pur*, a word derived from the Latin *porrum*, an onion, and picked up by the Gypsies in Roumania or Wallachia, the natives of which region speak a highly curious mixture of Latin and Sclavonian.

LOVEL. — This is the name or title of an old and powerful English family. The meaning of it is Leo's town, Lowe's town, or Louis' town. The Gypsies, who adopted it, seem to have imagined that it had something to do with love, for they translated it by *Camlo* or *Caumlo*, that which is lovely or amiable, and also by *Camomescro*, a lover, an amorous person, sometimes used for 'friend.' *Camlo* is connected with the Sanscrit *Cama*, which signifies love, and is the appellation of the Hindoo god of love. A name of the same root as the one borne by that divinity was not altogether inapplicable to the Gypsy tribe who adopted it: *Cama*, if all tales be true, was black, black though comely, a *Beltenebros*, and the Lovel tribe is decidedly the most comely and at the same time the darkest of all the Anglo-Egyptian families. The faces of many of them, male and female, are perfect specimens of black beauty. They are generally called by the race the *Kaulo Camloes*, the Black Comelies. And here, though at the risk of being thought digressive, the writer cannot forbear saying that the darkest and at one time the comeliest of all the *Caumlies*, a celebrated fortune-teller, and an old friend of his, lately expired in a certain old town, after attaining an age which was something wonderful. She had twenty-one brothers and sisters, and was the eldest of the family, on which account she was called "Rawnie P., pooroest of bis ta dui," Lady P. — she had married out of the family — eldest of twenty-two.

MARSHALL. — The name Marshall has either to do with marshal, the title of a high military personage, or marches, the borders of contiguous countries. In the early Norman period it was the name of an Earl of Pembroke. The Gypsies who adopted the name seem in translating it to have been of opinion that it was connected with marshes, for they rendered it by *mokkado tan engre*, fellows of the wet or miry place, an appellation which at one time certainly became them well, for they are a northern tribe belonging to the Border, a country not very long ago full of mosses and miry places. Though calling themselves English, they are in reality quite as much Scotch as English, and as often to be found in Scotland as the other country, especially in Dumfriesshire and Galloway, in which latter region, in Saint Cuthbert's churchyard, lies buried 'the old man' of the race, — Marshall, who died at the age of 107. They sometimes call themselves *Bungyoror* and *Chikkeneymengre*, cork-fellows and china people, which names have reference to the occupations severally followed by the maies and females, the former being cutters of bungs and corks, and the latter menders of china.

STANLEY. — This is the name or title of an ancient English family celebrated in history. It is probably descriptive of their original place of residence, for it signifies the stony lea, which is also the meaning of the Gaelic *Auchinlech*, the place of abode of the Scottish Boswells. It was adopted by an English Gypsy tribe, at one time very numerous, but at present much diminished. Of this name there are two renderings into Romany; one is *Baryor* or *Baremescre*, stone-folks or stone-masons, the other is *Beshaley*. The first requires no comment, but the second is well worthy of analysis, as it is an example of the strange blunders which the Gypsies sometimes make in their attempts at translation. When they rendered Stanley by *Beshaley* or *Beshley*, they mistook the first syllable *stan* for 'stand,' but for a very good reason rendered it by *besh*, which signifies 'to sit' and the second for a word in their own language, for *ley* or *aley* in Gypsy signifies 'down,' so they rendered Stanley by *Beshley* or *Beshaley*, which signifies 'sit down.' Here, of course, it will be asked what reason could have induced them, if they mistook *stan* for 'stand', not to have rendered it by the Gypsy word for 'stand'? The reason was a very cogent one, the want of a word in the Gypsy language to express 'stand'; but they had heard in courts of justice witnesses told to stand down, so they supposed that to stand down was much the same as to sit down, whence their odd rendering of Stanley. In no dialect of the Gypsy, from the Indus to the Severn, is there any word for 'stand,' though in every one there is a word for 'sit,' and that is *besh*, and in every Gypsy encampment all along the vast distance, *Beshley* or *Beshaley* would be considered an invitation to sit down.

So much for the double-name system in use among the Gypsies of England. There is something in connection with the Gypsies of Spain which strangely coincides with one part of it — the translation of names. Among the relics of the language of the Gitanos or Spanish Gypsies are words, some simple and some compound, which are evidently attempts to translate names in a manner corresponding to the plan employed by the English Romany. In illustration of the matter, the writer will give an analysis of *Brono Aljenicato*, the rendering into Gitano of the name of one frequently mentioned in the New Testament, and once in the Apostle's Creed, the highly respectable, but much traduced individual known to the English public as Pontius Pilate, to the Spanish as Poncio Pilato. The manner in which the rendering has been accomplished is as follows: *Poncio* bears some resemblance to the Spanish *puente*, which signifies a bridge, and is a modification of the Latin *pons*, and *Pilato* to the Spanish *pila*, a fountain, or rather a stone pillar, from the top of which the waters of a fountain springing eventually fall into a stone basin below, the two words — the *Brono Aljenicato* — signifying bridge-fountain, or that which is connected with such a thing. Now this is the identical, or all but the identical, way in which the names Lee, Lovel, and Stanley have been done into English Romany. A remarkable instance is afforded in this Gitano Scripture name, this *Brono Aljenicato*, of the heterogeneous materials of which Gypsy dialects are composed: *Brono* is a modification of a Hindoo or Sanscrit, *Aljenicato* of an Arabic root. *Brono* is connected with the Sanscrit *pindala*, which signifies a bridge, and *Aljenicato* is a modification of the Gypsy *aljenique*, derived from the Arabic *alain*, which signifies the fountain. But of whatever materials composed, a fine-sounding name is this same *Brono Aljenicato*, perhaps the finest sounding specimen of Spanish Gypsy extant, much finer than a translation of Pontius Pilate would be, provided the name served to express the same things, in English, which *Poncio Pilato* serves to express in Spanish, for then it would be *Pudjico Pani* or Bridgwater; for though in English Gypsy there is the word for a bridge, namely *pudge*, a modification of the Persian *pul*, or the Wallachian *podul*, there is none for a fountain, which can be only vaguely paraphrased by *pani*, water.

Fortune-Telling

Gypsy women, as long as we have known anything of Gypsy history, have been arrant fortune-tellers. They plied fortune-telling about France and Germany as early as 1414, the year when the dusky bands were first observed in Europe, and they have never relinquished the practice. There are two words for fortune-telling in Gypsy, *bocht* and *dukkering*. *Bocht* is a Persian word, a modification of, or connected with, the Sanscrit *bagya*, which signifies 'fate.' *Dukkering* is the modification of a Wallaco-Sclavonian word signifying something spiritual or ghostly. In Eastern European Gypsy, the Holy Ghost is called *Swentuno Ducos*.

Gypsy fortune-telling is much the same everywhere, much the same in Russia as it is in Spain and in England. Everywhere there are three styles — the lofty, the familiar, and the homely; and every Gypsy woman is mistress of all three, and uses each according to the rank of the person whose *vast* she *dukkers*, whose hand she reads, and adapts the luck she promises. There is a ballad of some antiquity in the Spanish language about the *Buena Ventura*, a few stanzas of which translated will convey a tolerable idea of the first of these styles to the reader, who will probably with no great reluctance dispense with any illustrations of the other two: —

> Late rather one morning
> In summer's sweet tide,
> Goes forth to the Prado
> Jacinta the bride:
>
> There meets her a Gypsy
> So fluent of talk,
> And jauntily dressed,
> On the principal walk

"O welcome, thrice welcome,
  Of beauty thou flower!
Believe me, believe me,
  Thou com'st in good hour."

Surprised was Jacinta;
  She fain would have fled;
But the Gypsy to cheer her
  Such honeyed words said:

"O cheek like the rose-leaf!
  O lady high-born!
Turn thine eyes on thy servant,
  But ah, not in scorn.

"O pride of the Prado!
  O joy of our crime!
Thou twice shalt be married,
  And happily each time.

"Of two noble sons
  Thou shalt be the glad mother,
One a Lord Judge,
  A Field-Marshal the other."

Gypsy females have told fortunes to higher people than the
young Countess Jacinta: *Modor* — of the Gypsy quire of
Moscow — told the fortune of Ekatarina, Empress of all the
Russias. The writer does not know what the Ziganka told that
exalted personage, but it appears that she gave perfect satis-
faction to the Empress, who not only presented her with a
diamond ring — a Russian diamond ring is not generally of
much value — but also her hand to kiss. The writer's old
friend, Pepíta, the Gitana of Madrid, told the *bahi* of
Christina, the Regentess of Spain, in which she assured her
that she would marry the son of the King of France and
received from the fair Italian a golden ounce, the most
magnificent of coins, a guerdon which she richly merited, for
she nearly hit the mark, for though Christina did not marry
the son of the King of France, her second daughter was
married to a son of the King of France, the Duke of M—, one
of the three claimants of the crown of Spain, and the best of
the lot; and Britannia, the Caumli, told the good luck to the

Regent George on Newmarket Heath, and received 'foive guineas' and a hearty smack from him who eventually became George the Fourth — no bad fellow by the by, either as regent or king, though as much abused as Pontius Pilate, whom he much resembled in one point, unwillingness to take life — the *sonkaypè* or gold-gift being, no doubt, more acceptable than the *choomapé* or kiss-gift to the Beltenebrosa, who, if a certain song be true, had no respect for *gorgios*, however much she liked their money: —

Britannia is my nav;
I am a Kaulo Camlo;
The gorgios pen I be
A bori chovahaunie;
And tatchipen they pens,
The dinneleskie gorgies,
For mande chovahans
The luvvu from their putsies.

Britannia is my name;
I am a swarthy Lovel;
The Gorgios say I be
A witch of wondrous power;
And faith they speak the truth,
The silly, foolish fellows,
For often I bewitch
The money from their pockets.

Fortune-telling in all countries where the Gypsies are found is frequently the prelude to a kind of trick called in all Gypsy dialects by something more or less resembling the Sanscrit *kuhana*; for instance, it is called in Spain *jojana, hokano*, and in English *hukni*. It is practised in various ways, all very similar; the defrauding of some simple person of money or property being the object in view. Females are generally the victims of the trick, especially those of the middle class, who are more accessible to *the poor woman* than those of the upper. One of the ways, perhaps the most artful, will be found described in another chapter.

THE HUKNI

The Gypsy makes some poor simpleton of a lady believe that if the latter puts her gold into her hands, and she makes it up into a parcel, and puts it between the lady's feather-bed and mattress, it will at the end of a month be multiplied a hundredfold, provided the lady does not look at it during all that time. On receiving the money she makes it up into a brown paper parcel, which she seals with wax, turns herself repeatedly round, squints, and spits, and then puts between the feather-bed and mattress — not the parcel of gold, but one exactly like it, which she has prepared beforehand, containing old halfpence, farthings, and the like; then, after cautioning the lady by no means to undo the parcel before the stated time, she takes her departure singing to herself: —

> O dear me! O dear me!
> What dinnelies these gorgies be.

The above artifice is called by the English Gypsies the *hukni*, and by the Spanish *hokhano baro*, or the great lie. *Hukni* and *hokano* were originally one and the same word; the root seems to be the Sanscrit *huhanā*, lie, trick, deceit.

CAURING

The Gypsy has some queer, old-fashioned gold piece; this she takes to some goldsmith's shop, at the window of which she has observed a basin full of old gold coins, and shows it to the goldsmith, asking him if he will purchase it. He looks at it attentively, and sees that it is of very pure gold; whereupon he says that he has no particular objection to buy it; but that as it is very old it is not of much value, and that he has several like it. "Have you indeed, Master?" says the Gypsy; "then pray show them to me, and I will buy them; for, to tell you the truth, I would rather buy than sell pieces like this, for I have a great respect for them, and know their value: give me back my coin, and I will compare any you have with it." The goldsmith gives her back her coin, takes his basin of gold from the window, and places it on the counter. The Gypsy puts down her head, and pries into the basin. "Ah, I see nothing here like my coin," says she. "Now, Master, to oblige me, take out a handful of the coins and lay them on the counter; I am a poor, honest woman, Master, and do not wish to put my hand into your basin. Oh! if I could find one coin like my own, I would give much money for it; *barributer* than it is worth." The goldsmith, to oblige the poor, simple, foreign creature (for such he believes her to be), and, with considerable hope of profit, takes a handful of coins from the basin and puts them upon the counter. "I fear there is none here like mine, Master," says the Gypsy, moving the coins rapidly with the tips of her fingers. "No, no, there is not one here like mine — *kek yeck, kek yeck* — not one, not one. Stay, stay! What's this, what's this? *So se cavo, so se cavo?* Oh, here is one like mine; or if not quite like, like enough to suit me. Now, Master, what will you take for this coin?" The goldsmith looks at it, and names a price considerably above the value; whereupon she says: "Now, Master, I will deal fairly with you: you have not asked me the full value of the coin by three three-groats, three-groats, three-groats; by *trin tringurushis, tringurushis, tringurushis*. So here's the money you asked, Master, and three three-groats, three shillings, besides. God bless you, Master! You would have cheated yourself, but the poor woman would not let you; for though she is poor she is honest": and thus she takes her leave, leaving the goldsmith very well satisfied with his customer — with little reason, however, for out of about twenty coins which he laid on the counter she had filched at least three, which her brown nimble fingers, though they seemingly scarcely touched the gold, contrived to convey up her sleeves. This kind of pilfering is called by the English Gypsies *cauring*, and by the Spanish *ustilar pastèsas*, or stealing with the fingers. The word *caur* seems to be connected with the English *cower*, and the Hewbrew *kāra*, a word of frequent occurrence in the historical part of the Old Testament, and signifying to bend, stoop down, *incurvare*.

Metropolitan Gypsyries

What may be called the grand Metropolitan Gypsyry is on the Surrey side of the Thames. Near the borders of Wandsworth and Battersea, about a quarter of a mile from the river, is an open piece of ground which may measure about two acres. To the south is a hill, at the foot of which is a railway, and it is skirted on the north by the Wandsworth and Battersea Road. This place is what the Gypsies call a *kekkeno mushes puv*, a no man's ground; a place which has either no proprietor, or which the proprietor, for some reason, makes no use of for the present. The houses in the neighbourhood are mean and squalid, and are principally inhabited by artisans of the lowest description. This spot, during a considerable portion of the year, is the principal place of residence of the Metropolitan Gypsies, and of other people whose manner of life more or less resembles theirs. During the summer and autumn the little plain, for such it is, is quite deserted, except that now and then a wretched tent or two may be seen upon it, belonging to some tinker family, who have put up there for a few hours on their way through the metropolis; for the Gypsies are absent during summer, some at fairs and races, the men with their cocoa-nuts and the women busy at fortune-telling, or at suburban places of pleasure — the former with their donkeys for the young cockneys to ride upon, and the latter as usual *dukkering* and *hokkering*, and the other travellers, as they are called, roaming about the country following their particular avocations, whilst in the autumn the greater part of them all are away in Kent, getting money by picking hops. As soon, however, as the rains, the precursors of winter, descend, the place begins to be occupied, and about a week or two before Christmas it is almost crammed with the tents and caravans of the wanderers; and then it is a place well worthy to be explored, notwithstanding the inconvenience of being up to one's ankles in mud, and the rather appalling risk of being bitten by the Gypsy and travelling dogs tied to the tents and caravans, in whose teeth there is always venom and sometimes that which can bring on the water-horror, for which no European knows a remedy. The following is an attempt to describe the odd people and things to be met with here; the true Gypsies, and what to them pertaineth, being of course noticed first.

On this plain there may be some fifteen or twenty Gypsy tents and caravans. Some of the tents are large, as indeed it is highly necessary that they should be being inhabited by large families — a man and his wife, a grandmother a sister or two and half a dozen children, being, occasionally found in one; some of them are very small, belonging to poor old females who have lost their husbands, and whose families have separated themselves from them, and allow them to shift for themselves. During the day the men are generally busy at their several avocations, *chinning the cost*, that is, cutting the stick for skewers, making pegs for linen-lines, *kipsimengring* or basket-making, tinkering or braziering; the children are playing about, or begging halfpence by the road of passengers; whilst the women are strolling about, either in London or the neighbourhood, engaged in fortune-telling or swindling. Of the trades of the men, the one by far the most practised is *chinning the cost*, and as they sit at the door of the tents, cutting and whittling away, they occasionally sweeten their toil by raising their voices and singing the Gypsy stanza in which the art is mentioned, and which for terseness and expressiveness is quite equal to anything in the whole circle of Gentile poetry:

> Can you rokra Romany?
>> Can you play the bosh?
> Can you jal adrey the staripen?
>> Can you chin the cost?

> *Can you speak the Roman tongue?*
>> *Can you play the fiddle?*
> *Can you eat the prison-loaf?*
>> *Can you cut and whittle?*

These Gypsies are of various tribes, but chiefly Purruns, Chumomescroes and Vardomescroes, or Lees, Boswells and Coopers, and Lees being by far the most numerous. The men are well made, active fellows, somewhat below the middle height. Their complexions are dark, and their eyes are full of intelligence; their habiliments are rather ragged. The women are mostly wild-looking creatures, some poorly clad, others exhibiting not a little strange finery. There are some truly singular beings amongst those women, which is more than can be said with respect to the men, who are much on a level, and amongst whom there is none whom it is possible to bring prominently out, and about whom much can be said. The women, as has been already observed, are generally out during the day, being engaged in their avocations abroad. There is a very small tent about the middle of the place; it belongs to a lone female, whom one frequently meets wandering about Wandsworth or Battersea, seeking an opportunity to *dukker* some credulous servant-girl. It is hard that she should have to do so, as she is more than seventy-five years of age, but if she did not she would probably starve. She is very short of statue, being little more than five feet and an inch high, but she is wonderfully strongly built. Her head is very large, and seems to have been placed at once upon her shoulders without any interposition of neck. Her face is broad, with a good-humoured expression upon it and in general with very little vivacity; at times however, it lights up, and then all the Gypsy beams forth. Old as she is, her hair, which is very long, is as black as the plumage of a crow and she walks sturdily, though with not much elasticity, on her short, thick legs, and, if requested, would take up the heaviest man in Wandsworth or Battersea and walk away with him. She is, upon the whole, the oddest Gypsy woman ever seen; see her once and you will never forget her. Who is she? you ask. Who is she? Why, Mrs. Cooper, the wife of Jack Cooper, the fighting Gypsy, once the terror of all the Light Weights of the English Ring; who knocked West Country Dick to pieces, and killed Paddy O'Leary, the fighting pot-boy, Jack Randall's pet. Ah, it would have been well for Jack if he had always stuck to his true, lawful Romany wife, whom at one time he was very fond of, and whom he used to dress in silks and satins, and best scarlet cloth, purchased with the money gained in his fair, gallant battles in the Ring! But he did not stick to her, deserting her for a painted Jezebel, to support whom he sold his battles, by doing which he lost his friends and backers; then took from his poor wife all he had given her, and even plundered her of her own property, down to the very blankets which she lay upon; and who finally was so infatuated with love for his paramour that he bore the blame of a crime which she had committed, and in which he had no share, suffering ignominy and transportation in order to save her. Better had he never deserted his *tatchie romadie*, his own true Charlotte, who, when all deserted him, the painted Jezebel being the first to do so, stood by him, supporting him with money in prison, and feeing counsel on his trial from the scanty proceeds of her *dukkering*. All that happened many years ago; Jack's term of transportation, a lengthy one, has long, long been expired, but he has not come back, though every year since the expiration of his servitude he has written her a letter, or caused one to be written to her, to say that he is coming, that he is coming; so that she is always expecting him, and is at all times willing, as she says, to re-invest him with all the privileges of a husband, and to beg and *dukker* to support him if necessary. A true wife she has been to him, a *tatchie romadie*, and has never taken up with any man since he left her, though many have been the tempting offers that she has had, connubial offers, notwithstanding the oddity of her appearance. Only one wish she has now in this world, the wish that he may return; but her wish, it is to be feared, is a vain one, for Jack lingers and lingers in the *Sonnakye Tem*, golden Australia, teaching, it is said, the young Australians to box, tempted by certain shining nuggets, the produce of the golden region. It is pleasant, though there is something mournful in it, to visit Mrs. Cooper after nightfall, to sit with her in her little tent after she has taken her cup of tea, and is warming her tired limbs at her little coke fire, and hear her talk of old times and things: how Jack courted her 'neath the trees of Loughton Forest, and how, when tired of courting, they would get up and box, and how he occasionally gave her a black eye, and how she invariably flung him at a close; and how they were lawfully married at church, and what a nice man the clergyman was, and what funny things he said both before and after he had united them; how stoutly West Country Dick contended against Jack, though always losing; how in Jack's battle with Paddy O'Leary the Irishman's head in the last round was truly frightful, not a feature being distinguishable, and one of his ears hanging down by a bit of skin; how Jack vanquished Hardy Scroggins, whom Jack Randall himself never dared fight. Then, again, her anecdotes of Alec Reed, cool, swift-hitting Alec, who was always smiling, and whose father was a Scotchman, his mother an Irishwoman, and who was born in Guernsey; and of Oliver, old Tom Oliver, who seconded Jack in all his winning battles, and after whom he named his son, his only child, Oliver, begotten of her in lawful wedlock, a good and affectionate son enough, but unable to assist her, on account of his numerous family. Farewell, Mrs. Cooper, true old Charlotte! here's a little bit of silver for you, and a little bit of a *gillie* to sing:

> Charlotta is my nav,
> I am a puro Purrun;
> My romado was Jack,
> The couring Vardomescro.
> He muk'd me for a lubbeny,
> Who chor'd a rawnie's kissi;
> He penn'd 'twas he who lell'd it,
> And so was bitched pawdel.

> *Old Charlotte I am called,*
> *Of Lee I am a daughter;*
> *I married Fighting Jack,*
> *The famous Gypsy Cooper.*
> *He left me for a harlot,*
> *Who pick'd a lady's pocket;*
> *He bore the blame to save her,*
> *And so was sent to Bot'ny.*

Just within the bounds of the plain, and close by the road, may occasionally be seen a small caravan of rather a neat appearance. It comes and goes suddenly, and is seldom seen there for more than three days at a time. It belongs to a Gypsy female who, like Mrs. Cooper, is a remarkable person, but is widely different from Mrs. Cooper in many respects.

Mrs. Cooper certainly does not represent the *beau ideal* of a Gypsy female, this does — a dark, mysterious, beautiful, terrible creature! She is considerably above the middle height, powerfully but gracefully made, and about thirty-seven years of age. Her face is oval, and of a dark olive. The nose is Grecian, the cheek-bones rather high; the eyes somewhat sunk, but of a lustrous black; the mouth small, and the teeth exactly like ivory. Upon the whole the face is exceedingly beautiful, but the expression is evil — evil to a degree. Who she is no one exactly knows, nor what is her name, nor whether she is single woman, wife, or widow. Some say she is a foreign Gypsy, others from Scotland, but she is neither — her accent is genuine English. What strikes one as most singular is the power she possesses of appearing in various characters — all Romany ones it is true, but so different as seemingly to require three distinct females of the race to represent them: sometimes she is the staid, quiet, respectable Gypsy; sometimes the forward and impudent; at others the awful and sublime. Occasionally you may see her walking the streets dressed in a black silk gown, with a black silk bonnet on her head; over her left arm is flung a small carpet, a sample of the merchandise which is in her caravan, which is close at hand, driven by a brown boy; her address to her customers is highly polite; the tones of her voice are musical, though somewhat deep. At Fairlop, on the first Friday of July, in the evening, she may be found near the Bald-faced Hind, dressed in a red cloak and a large beaver; her appearance is bold and reckless — she is *dukkering* low tradesmen and servant girls behind the trees at sixpence a head, or is bandying with the voice of a raven slang and obscenity with country boors, or with the blackguard butcher-boys who throng in from Whitechapel and Shoreditch to the Gypsy Fair. At Goodwood, a few weeks after, you may see her in a beautiful half-riding dress, her hair fantastically plaited and adorned with pearls, standing beside the carriage of a Countess, telling the fortune of her ladyship with the voice and look of a pythoness. She is a thing of incongruities; an incomprehensible being! nobody can make her out; the writer himself has tried to make her out but could not, though he has spoken to her in his deepest Romany. It is true there is a certain old Gypsy, a friend of his, who thinks he has made her out. "Brother," said he one day, "why you should be always going after that woman I can't conceive, unless indeed you have lost your wits. If you go after her for her Romany you will find yourself in the wrong box: she may have a crumb or two of Romany, but for every crumb that she has I am quite sure you have a quartern loaf. Then as for her beauty, of which it is true she has plenty, and for which half a dozen Gorgios that I knows of are running mad, it's of no use going after her for that, for her beauty she keeps for her own use and that of her master the Devil; not but that she will sell it — she's sold it a dozen times to my certain knowledge — but what's the use of buying a thing, when the fool who buys it never gets it, never has the 'joyment of it, brother? She is *kek tatcho*, and that's what I like least in her; there's no trusting her, neither Gorgio nor Romano can trust her: she sells her *truppos* to a Rye-gorgio for five *bars*, and when she has got them, and the Gorgio, as he has a right to do, begins to *kelna lasa*, she laughs and asks him if he knows whom he has to deal with; then if he *lels bonnek of lati*, as he is quite justified in doing, she whips out a *churi*, and swears if he doesn't leave off she will stick it in his *gorlo*. Oh! she's an evil mare, a *wafodu grasni*, though a handsome one, and I never looks at her, brother, without saying to myself the old words:

> "Rinkeno mui and wafodu zee
> Kitzi's the cheeros we dicks cattanē."

> *A beautiful face and a black wicked mind*
> *Often, full often together we find.*

Some more particular account than what has been already given of the habitations of these Wandsworth Gypsies, and likewise of their way of life, will perhaps not be unacceptable here.

To begin with the tents. They are oblong in shape and of very simple construction, whether small or great. Sticks or rods, called in the Gypsy language *ranior*, between four and five feet in length, and *croming* or bending towards the top are stuck in the ground at about twenty inches from each other, a rod or two being omitted in that part where the entrance is intended to be. The *cromes* or bends serve as supporters of a roof, and those of the side rods which stand over against one another are generally tied together by strings. These rods are covered over with coarse brown cloths, pinned or skewered together; those at the bottom being fastened to the ground by pegs. Around the tent is generally a slight embankment, about two or three inches high, or a little trench about the same depth, to prevent water from running into the tent in time of rain. Such is the tent, which would be exactly like the Indian wigwam but for the cloth which forms the covering: the Indians in lieu of cloth using bark, which they carry about with them in all their migrations, though they leave the sticks standing in the ground.

The furniture is scanty. Like the Arabs, the Gypsies have neither chairs nor tables, but sit cross-legged, a posture which is perfectly easy to them, though insufferable to a Gorgio, unless he happens to be a tailor. When they eat, the ground serves them for a board, though they occasionally spread a cloth upon it. Singularly enough, though they have neither chairs nor tables, they have words for both. Of pots, pans, plates, and trenchers, they have a tolerable quantity. Each grown-up person has a *churi*, or knife with which to cut food. Eating-forks they have none, and for an eating-fork they have no word, the term *pusengri* signifying a straw- or pitch-fork. Spoons are used by them generally of horn, and are called *royis*. They have but two culinary articles, the *kekkauvi* and *pirry*, kettle and boiler, which are generally of copper, to which, however, may perhaps be added the *kekkauviskey saster*, or kettle-iron, by which the kettle and boiler are hung over the fire. As a fireplace they have a large iron pan on three legs, with holes or eyes in the sides, in order that the heat of the fire may be cast around. Instead of coals they use coke, which emits no flame and little smoke, and casts a considerable heat. Every tent has a pail or two, and perhaps a small cask or barrel, the proper name for which is *bedra*, though it is generally called *pāni-mengri*, or thing for water. At the farther end of the tent is a mattress, with a green cloth, or perhaps a sheet spread upon it, forming a kind of couch, on which visitors are generally asked to sit down: — *Av adrey, Romany Rye, av adrey ta besh aley pawdle odoy!* Come in,

Gypsy gentleman (said a polite Gypsy one day to the writer); come in and sit down over yonder! They have a box or two in which they stow away their breakable articles and whatever things they set any particular value upon. Some of them have small feather-beds, and they are generally tolerably well provided with blankets.

The caravans are not numerous, and have only been used of late years by any of the English Gypsy race. The caravan called by the Gypsies *keir vardo*, or waggon-house, is on four wheels, and is drawn by a horse or perhaps a couple of donkeys. It is about twelve feet long by six broad and six high. At the farther end are a couple of transverse berths, one above the other, like those in the cabin of a ship; and a little way from these is a curtain hanging by rings from an iron rod running across, which, when drawn, forms a partition. On either side is a small glazed window. The most remarkable object is a stove just inside the door, on the left hand, with a metal chimney which goes through the roof. This stove, the Gypsy term for which is *bo*, casts, when lighted, a great heat, and in some cases is made in a very handsome fashion. Some caravans have mirrors against the sides, and exhibit other indications of an aiming at luxury, though in general they are dirty, squalid places, quite as much as or perhaps more than the tents, which seem to be the proper and congenial homes of the Gypsies.

The mode of life of these people may be briefly described. They have two regular meals — breakfast and supper. The breakfast consists of tea, generally of the best quality, bread, butter, and cheese; the supper, of tea and a stew. In spring time they occasionally make a kind of tea or soup of the tender leaves of a certain description of nettle. This preparation, which they call *dandri-mengreskie zimmen*, or the broth of the stinging-thing, is highly relished by them. They get up early, and go to bed betimes. After breakfast the men sit down to *chin the cost*, to mend chairs or make baskets; the women go forth to *hok* and *dukker*, and the children to beg, or to go with the donkeys to lanes and commons to watch them, whilst they try to fill their poor bellies with grass and thistles. These children sometimes bring home *hotchi-witches*, or hedgehogs, the flesh of which is very sweet and tender, and which their mothers are adepts at cooking.

The Gypsies, as has been already observed, are not the sole occupiers of Wandsworth grounds. Strange, wild guests are to be found there, who without being Gypsies, have much of Gypsyism in their habits, and who far exceed the Gypsies in number. To pass them by without notice would be unpardonable. They may be divided into three classes: Chorodies, Kora-mengre, and Hindity-mengre. Something about each: —

The Chorodies are the legitimate descendants of the rogues and outcasts who roamed about England long before its soil was trodden by a Gypsy foot. They are a truly detestable set of beings; both men and women being ferocious in their appearance, and in their conversation horrible and disgusting. They have coarse, vulgar features, and hair which puts one wonderfully in mind of refuse flax, or the material of which mops are composed. Their complexions, when not obscured with grime, are rather fair than dark, evidencing that their origin is low, swinish Saxon, and not gentle Romany. Their language is the frowsiest English, interlarded with cant expressions and a few words of bastard Romany. They live in the vilest tents, with the exception of two or three families, who have their abode in broken and filthy caravans. They have none of the comforts and elegancies of the Gypsies. They are utterly destitute of civility and good manners, and are generally squalid in their dress, though the women sometimes exhibit not a little dirty tawdriness. The trades of the men are tinkering and basket-making, and some few "peel the stick." The women go about with the articles made by their husbands, or rather partners, and sometimes do a little in the fortune-telling line — pretty prophetesses! The fellows will occasionally knock a man down in the dark and rob him; the women will steal anything they can conveniently lay their hands on. Singular as it may seem to those not deeply acquainted with human nature, these wretches are not without a kind of pride. "We are no Gypsies — not we! no, nor Irish either. We are English, and decent folks — none of your rubbish!" The Gypsies hold them, and with reason, in supreme contempt, and it is from them that they got their name of Chorodies, not a little applicable to them. *Choredo*, in Gypsy, signifies a poor, miserable person, and differs very little in sound from two words, one Sanscrit and the other

Hebrew, both signifying, like the Gypsy term, something low, mean, and contemptible.

Kora-mengre are the lowest of those hawkers who go about the country villages and the streets of London, with caravans hung about with various common articles, such as mats, brooms, mops, tin pans and kettles. These low hawkers seem to be of much the same origin as the Chorodies, and are almost equally brutal and repulsive in their manners. The name Kora-mengre is Gypsy, and signifies fellows who cry out and shout, from their practice of shouting out the names of their goods. The word *kora*, or *karra*, is by no means bad Hebrew: *kora*, in the Holy Language, signifies he cried out, called, or proclaimed; and a partridge is called in Hebrew *kora*, from its continually crying out to its young, when leading them about to feed. *Koran*, the name of the sacred book of the Mahomedans, is of the same root.

Lastly come the Hindity-mengre, or Filthy People. This term has been bestowed upon the vagrant Irish by the Gypsies, from the dirty ways attributed to them, though it is a question whether the lowest Irish are a bit more dirty in their ways than the English Chorodies, or indeed so much, and are certainly immeasurably superior to them in many respects. There are not many of them here, seldom more than two families, and sometimes, even during the winter, not a single Irish tent or cart is to be seen. The trade they ostensibly drive is tinkering, repairing old kettles, and making little pots and pans of tin. The one, however, on which they principally depend, is not tinkering, but one far more lucrative, and requiring more cleverness and dexterity; they make false rings, like the Gypsy smiths, the *fashiono vangust-engre* of old, and whilst speaking Celtic to one whom they deem their countryman, have no hesitation in acknowledging themselves to be "Cairdean droich oir," workers of false gold. The rings are principally made out of old brass buttons; those worn by old Chelsea pensioners being considered the very best for the purpose. Many an ancient Corporal Trim, after having spent all his money at the public-house, and only become three-parts boozy, has been induced by the Hindity-mengro to sell all his buttons at the rate of three-halfpence a-piece, in order to have wherewithal to make himself thoroughly royal. Each of these Hindity-mengre has his blow-pipe, and some of them can execute their work in a style little inferior to that of a first-rate working goldsmith. The rings, after being made, are rubbed with a certain stuff out of a phial, which gives them all the appearance of gold. This appearance, however, does not long endure, for after having been worn two or three months, the ring loses its false appearance entirely, and any one can see that it is worthless metal. A good many of these rings are disposed of at good prices by the Hindity women, the wives of these false-gold workers, to servant girls and the wives of small shopkeepers, and not a few, at a lower rate, to certain gentry who get their livelihood by the honourable profession of *ring-dropping*.

What is ring-dropping?

Ring-dropping is this. A gentleman overtakes you as you are walking in some quiet street, passes by you, and at the distance of some fifteen yards stops, and stooping down, seemingly picks up something, which he inspects, and then uttering a "Dear me!" he turns to you, and says, "Sir, we have been fortunate to-day. See! I have picked up this valuable!" He then shows you a small case, in which is a large ring, seemingly of the finest gold, with a little label attached to it, on which is marked £2 15s. "Now, sir," he continues, "I said *we* were fortunate, because as we were close to each other, I consider you as much entitled to gain by this windfall as myself. I'll tell you how it shall be: the price of the ring, which was probably dropped by some goldsmith's man, is, as you see, two pound fifteen; however, as I am in a hurry, you shall only give me a quid, a pound, and then the valuable shall be all your own; it shall indeed, sir!" And then he stares you in the face. Such is ring-dropping, to which many silly but greedy individuals, fall victims; giving a pound for a fine-looking ring, which, however, with its scarlet case — for the case is always of a scarlet colour — is not worth sixpence. The best thing you can do in such a case is to put your thumb to your nose, flattening your hand and sticking out your fingers far apart, moving on at the same time, or to utter the cabalistic word "hookey"; in either case the ring-dropper will at once drop astern, with a half-stifled curse, for he knows that he has to do with "no flat," and that you are "awake to his little game." Doing so is much better than moving rapidly on, and affecting to take no notice of him, for then he will infallibly follow you to the end of the street, offering you the ring on more reasonable terms at every step, perhaps concluding at last, as a ring-dropper once did to the writer, "I'll tell you what, sir; as I am in a hurry, and rather hard up, you shall have the valuable for a bull, for a crown; you shall indeed, sir, so help me —"

Three of the most famous of the Hindity smiths have been immortalised by the Gypsies in the following bit of verse:

> Mickie, Huwie and Larry,
> Trin Hindity-mengre fashiono vangust-engre.

> *Mickie, Huwie and Larry bold,*
> *Three Irish brothers, as I am told,*
> *Who make false rings, that pass for gold.*

Of these *fashiono-vangust* brothers, the most remarkable is Mike — Old Mike, as he is generally called. He was born in the county Kerry, and educated at a hedge-school, where he learned to read and write English, after a fashion, and acquired the seventeen letters of the Irish alphabet, each of which is named after a particular tree. Leaving school he was apprenticed to a blacksmith, from whom he ran away, and enlisted into the service of that illustrious monarch, George the Third, some of whose battles he had the honour of fighting in the Peninsula and France. Discharged from the army at the Peace, with the noble donation of thirty shillings, or one month's pay, he returned to Ireland, took to himself a wife, and commenced tinker. Becoming dissatisfied with his native soil he passed over to England, and settling for some time at "Brummagem," took lessons from certain cunning smiths in the art of making *fashiono vangusties*. The next forty years of his life he spent in wandering about Britain, attended by his faithful partner, who not only disposed of his tin articles and false rings, but also bore him seventeen children all of whom are alive, somewhere or other, and thriving too, one of them indeed having attained to the dignity of American senator. Some of his adventures, during his wanderings, were in the highest degree extraordinary. Of late years he has chiefly resided in the vicinity of London, spending his winters at Wandsworth, and his summers on the

Flats, near Epping Forest; in one or the other of which places you may see Old Mike on a Sunday evening, provided the weather is tolerably fine, seated near his little caravan, with his wife by his side — not the wife who bore him the seventeen children, who has been dead for some years, but his second wife, a nice, elderly Irish *ban* from the county of Cork, who can tell fortunes, say her prayers in Irish, and is nearly as good a hand at selling her lord and master's tin articles and false rings as her predecessor. Lucky for Mike that he got such a second partner! and luckier still that at his age of seventy-nine he retains all his faculties, and is able to work for his daily bread, with at least the skill and cunning of his two brothers, both of whom are much younger men than himself, whose adventures have been somewhat similar to his own, and who, singularly enough, have come to live near him in his latter days. Both these brothers are highly remarkable men. Huwie is the most civil-spoken person in or about London, and Larry a man of the most terrible tongue, and perhaps the most desperate fighter ever seen; always willing to attack half a dozen men, if necessary, and afraid of no one in the world, save one — Mike, old Mike, who can tame him in his fiercest moods by merely holding up his finger. Oh, a truly remarkable man is old Mike! and a pleasure and an advantage it is to any one of a philosophical mind to be acquainted with him, and to listen to him. He is much more than a *fashiono-vangust-engro*. Amongst other things he is a theologian — Irish theologian — and quite competent to fill the chair of theology at the University of Maynooth. He can tell you a great many things connected with a certain person, which, with all your research, you would never find in Scripture. He can tell you how the Saviour, when hanging on the cross, became athirst, and told St. Peter, who stood at the foot of it, to fetch Him a cup of water from a dirty puddle in the neighbourhood, and how St. Peter — however, better not relate the legend, though a highly curious one. Then he can repeat to you blessed verses, as he calls them, by dozens; not of David, but of one quite as good, as he will tell you, namely, Timothy O'Sullivan; and who, you will say, was Timothy O'Sullivan? Why, Ty Gaelach, to be sure. And who was Ty Gaelach? An Irish peasant-poet of the last century, who wrote spiritual songs, some of them by no means bad ones, and who was called Gaelach, or Gael, from his abhorrence of the English race and of the English language, of which he scarcely understood a word. Then is Ty Irish for Timothy? Why, no! though very stupidly supposed to be so. Ty is Teague, which is neither Greek nor Irish, but a glorious old Northern name, carried into Ireland by the brave old heathen Danes. Ty or Teague is the same as Tycho. Ty or Teague Gaelach is as much as to say Tycho Gaelach; and Tycho Brahe is as much as to say Teague Brahe.

THE POTTERIES, 1864

The second great Gypsyry is on the Middlesex side of the river, and is distant about three miles, as the crow flies, from that of Wandsworth. Strange as it may seem, it is not far distant from the most fashionable part of London; from the beautiful squares, noble streets, and thousand palaces of Tyburnia, a region which, though only a small part of the enormous metropolis, can show more beautiful edifices, wealth, elegance, and luxury, than all foreign capitals put together. After passing Tyburnia, and going more than halfway down Notting Hill, you turn to the right, and proceed along a tolerably genteel street till it divides into two, one of which looks more like a lane than a street, and which is on the left hand, and bears the name of Pottery Lane. Go along this lane, and you will presently find yourself amongst a number of low, uncouth-looking sheds, open at the sides, and containing an immense quantity of earthen chimney-pots, pantiles, fancy-bricks, and similar articles. This place is called the Potteries, and gives the name of Pottery Lane to the lane through which you have just passed. A dirty little road goes through it, which you must follow, and presently turning to your left, you will enter a little, filthy street, and going some way down it, you will see, on your right hand, a little, open bit of ground, chock-full of crazy, battered caravans of all colours — some yellow, some green, some red. Dark men, wild-looking, witch-like women, and yellow-faced children are at the doors of the caravans, or wending their way through the narrow spaces left for transit between the vehicles. You have now arrived at the second grand Gypsyry of London — you are amongst the Romany Chals of the Potteries, called in Gypsy the *Koromengreskoe Tan*, or the place of the fellows who make pots; in which place certain Gypsies have settled, not with the view of making pots, an employment which they utterly eschew, but simply because it is convenient to them, and suits their fancy.

A goodly collection of Gypsies you will find in that little nook, crowded with caravans. Most of them are Tatchey Romany, real Gypsies, "long-established people, of the old order." Amongst them are Ratzie-mescroes, Hearnes, Herons, or duck-people; Chumo-mescroes or Bosvils; a Kaulo Camlo (a Black Lovel) or two, and a Beshaley or Stanley. It is no easy thing to find a Stanley nowadays, even in the Baulo Tem, or Hampshire, which is the proper home of the Stanleys, for the Bugnior, pimples or small-pox, has of late years made sad havoc amongst the Stanleys; but yonder tall old gentlewoman, descending the steps of a caravan, with a flaming red cloak and a large black beaver bonnet, and holding a travelling basket in her hand, is a Tatchey Beshaley, a "genuine" Stanley. The generality, however, of "them Gyptians" are Ratzie-mescroes, Hearnes, or duck-people; and, speaking of the Hearnes, it is but right to say that he who may be called the Gypsy Father of London, old Thomas Ratzie-mescro, or Hearne, though not exactly residing here, lives close by in a caravan, in a little bit of a yard over the way, where he can breathe more freely, and be less annoyed by the brats and the young fellows than he would be in yonder crowded place.

Though the spot which it has just been attempted to describe, may be considered as the head-quarters of the London Gypsies, on the Middlesex side of the Thames, the whole neighbourhood, for a mile to the north of it, may to a certain extent be considered a Gypsy region — that is, a district where Gypsies, or gentry whose habits very much resemble those of Gypsies, may at any time be found. No metropolitan district, indeed, could be well more suited for Gypsies to take up their abode in. It is a neighbourhood of transition; of brickfields, open spaces, poor streets inhabited by low artisans, isolated houses, sites of intended tenements, or sites of tenements which have been pulled down; it is in fact a mere chaos, where there is nothing durable, or intended to be durable; though there can be little doubt that within a few years order and beauty itself will be found here, that the misery, squalidness, and meanness will have disappeared, and the whole district, up to the railroad arches which bound it on the west and north, will be covered with palaces, like those of Tyburnia, or delightful villas, like those which decorate what is called Saint John's Wood. At present, however, it is quite the kind of place to please the Gypsies and wandering people, who find many places within its bounds where they can squat and settle, or take up their quarters for a night or two without much risk of being interfered with. Here their tents, cars, and caravans may be seen amidst ruins, half-raised walls, and on patches of unenclosed ground; here their children may, throughout the day, be seen playing about, flinging up dust and dirt, some partly naked, and others entirely so; and here, at night, the different families, men, women, and children, may be seen seated around their fires and their kettles, taking their evening meal, and every now and then indulging in shouts of merriment, as much as to say, —

What care we, though we be so small?
The tent shall stand when the palace shall fall;

which is quite true. The Gypsy tent must make way for the palace, but after a millennium or two, the Gypsy tent is pitched on the ruins of the palace.

Of the open spaces above mentioned, the most considerable is one called Latimer's Green. It lies on the north-western side of the district, and is not far from that place of old renown called the Shepherd's Bush, where in the good ancient times highwaymen used to lurk for the purpose of pouncing upon the travellers of the Oxford Road. It may contain about five or six acres, and, though nominally under the control of trustees, is in reality little more than a "no man's ground," where anybody may feed a horse, light a fire, and boil a kettle. It is a great resort of vagrant people, less of Gypsies than those who call themselves travellers, and are denominated by the Gypsies Chorodies, and who live for the most part in miserable caravans, though there is generally a Gypsy tent or two to be seen there, belonging to some

Deighton or Shaw, or perhaps Petulengro, from the Lil-engro Tan, as the Romany call Cambridgeshire. Amidst these Chorody caravans and Gypsy tents may frequently be seen the *ker-vardo*, the house on wheels, of one who, whenever he takes up his quarters here, is considered the cock of the walk, the king of the place. He is a little under forty years of age, and somewhat under five feet ten inches in height. His face is wonderfully like that of a mastiff of the largest size, particularly in its jowls; his neck is short and very thick, and must be nearly as strong as that of a bull; his chest is so broad that one does not like to say how broad it is; and the voice which every now and then proceeds from it has much the sound of that of the mighty dog just mentioned; his arms are long and exeedingly muscular, and his fists huge and bony. He wears a low-crowned, broad-brimmed hat, a coarse blue coat with short skirts, leggings, and high-lows. Such is the *kral o' the tan*, the *rex loci*, the cock of the green. But what is he besides? Is he Gypsy, *Chorody*, or *Hindity mush*? I say, you had better not call him by any one of those names, for if you did he would perhaps hit you, and then, oh dear! That is Mr. G. A., a travelling horse-dealer, who lives in a caravan, and finds it frequently convenient to take up his abode for weeks together on Latimer's Green. He is a thorough-bred Englishman, though he is married to a daughter of one of the old, sacred Gypsy families, a certain Lurina Ratziemescri, duck or heron female, who is a very handsome woman, and who has two brothers, dark, stealthy-looking young fellows, who serve with almost slavish obedience their sister's lord and husband, listening uncomplainingly to his abuse of Gypsies, whom, though he lives amongst them and is married to one by whom he has several children, he holds in supreme contempt, never speaking of them but as a lying, thievish, cowardly set, any three of whom he could beat with one hand; as perhaps he could, for he is a desperate pugilist, and has three times fought in "the ring" with good men, whom, though not a scientific fighter, he beat with ease by dint of terrible blows, causing them to roar out. He is very well to do in the world; his caravan, a rather stately affair, is splendidly furnished within; and it is a pleasure to see his wife, at Hampton Court races, dressed in Gypsy fashion, decked with real gems and jewels and rich gold chains, and waited upon by her dark brothers dressed like dandy pages. How is all this expense supported? Why, by horsedealing. Mr. G. is, then, up to all kinds of horsedealers' tricks, no doubt. Aye, aye, he is up to them, but he doesn't practise them. He says it's of no use, and that honesty is the best policy, and he'll stick to it; and so he does, and finds the profit of it. His traffic in horses, though confined entirely to small people, such as market-gardeners, travellers, show-folks, and the like, is very great; every small person who wishes to buy a horse, or to sell a horse, or to swop a horse, goes to Mr. G., and has never reason to complain, for all acknowledge that he has done the fair thing by them; though all agree that there is no over-reaching him, which indeed very few people try to do, deterred by the dread of his manual prowess, of which a Gypsy once gave to the writer the following *striking* illustration: — "He will jal oprey to a gry that's wafodu, prawla, and coure leste tuley with the courepen of his wast." (He will go up to a vicious horse, brother, and knock him down with a blow of his fist).

The arches of the railroad which bounds this region on the west and north serve as a resort for Gypsies, who erect within them their tents, which are thus sheltered in summer from the scorching rays of the sun, and in winter from the drenching rain. In what close proximity we sometimes find emblems of what is most rude and simple, and what is most artificial and ingenious! For example, below the arch is the Gypsy donkey-cart, whilst above it is thundering the chariot of fire which can run across a county in half an hour. The principal frequenters of these arches are Bosvils and Lees; the former are chiefly tinkers, and the latter *esconyemengres*, or skewer-makers. The reason for this difference is that the Bosvils are chiefly immigrants from the country, where there is not much demand for skewers, whereas the Lees are natives of the metropolis or the neighbourhood, where the demand for skewers has from time immemorial been enormously great. It was in the shelter of one of these arches that the celebrated Ryley Bosvil, the Gypsy king of Yorkshire, breathed his last a few years ago.

THE MOUNT

Before quitting the subject of Metropolitan Gypsies there is another place to which it will be necessary to devote a few words, though it is less entitled to the appelation of Gypsyry than rookery. It is situated in the East of London, a region far more interesting to the ethnologist and the philologist than the West, for there he will find people of all kinds of strange races, — the wildest Irish; Greeks, both Orthodox and Papistical; Jews, not only Ashkenazim and Sephardim, but even Karaite; the worst, and consequently the most interesting, description of Germans, the sugar-bakers; lots of Malays; plenty of Chinamen; two or three dozen Hottentots, and about the same number of Gypsies, reckoning men, woman, and children. Of the latter, and their place of abode, we have now only to do, leaving the other strange, odd people to be disposed of on some other occasion.

Not far from Shoreditch Church, and at a short distance from the street called Church Street, on the left hand, is a locality called Friars' Mount, but generally for shortness called The Mount. It derives its name from a friary built upon a small hillock in the time of Popery, where a set of fellows lived in laziness and luxury on the offerings of foolish and superstitious people, who resorted thither to kiss and worship an ugly wooden image of the Virgin, said to be a first-rate stick at performing miraculous cures. The neighbourhood, of course, soon became a resort for vagabonds of every description, for wherever friars are found rogues and thieves are sure to abound; and about Friars' Mount, highwaymen, coiners, and Gypsies dwelt in safety under the protection of the ministers of the miraculous image. The friary has long since disappeared, the Mount has been levelled, and the locality built over. The vice and villainy, however, which the friary called forth still cling to the district. It is one of the vilest dens of London, a grand resort for housebreakers, garotters, passers of bad money, and other disreputable people, though not for Gypsies; for however favourite a place it may have been for the Romany in the old time, it no longer finds much favour in their sight, from its not affording open spaces where they can pitch their tents. One very small street, however, is certainly entitled to the name of a Gypsy street, in which a few Gypsy families have always found it convenient to reside, and who are in the habit of receiving and lodging their brethren passing through London to and from Essex and other counties east of the metropolis. There is something peculiar in the aspect of this street, not observable in that of any of the others, which one who visits it, should he have been in Triana of Seville, would at once recognise as having seen in the aspect of the lanes and courts of that grand location of the Gypsies of the Andalusian capital.

The Gypsies of the Mount live much in the same manner as their brethren in the other Gypsyries of London. They *chin the cost*, make skewers, baskets, and let out donkeys for hire. The chief difference consists in their living in squalid houses, whilst the others inhabit dirty tents and caravans. The last Gypsy of any note who resided in this quarter was Joseph Lee; here he lived for a great many years, and here he died, having attained the age of ninety. During his latter years he was generally called Old Joe Lee, from his great age. His wife or partner, who was also exceedingly old, only survived him a few days. They were buried in the same grave, with much Gypsy pomp, in the neighbouring churchyard. They were both of pure Gypsy blood, and were generally known as the Gypsy king and queen of Shoreditch. They left a numerous family of children and grandchildren, some of whom are still to be found at the Mount. This old Joe Lee in his day was a celebrated horse and donkey witch — that is, he professed secrets which enabled him to make any wretched animal of either species exhibit for a little time the spirit and speed of "a flying drummedary." He was illustriously related, and was very proud on that account, especially in being the brother's son of old James, the *cauring mush*, whose exploits in the filching line will be remembered as long as the venerable tribe of Purrum, or Lee, continues in existence.

Ryley Bosvil

Ryley Bosvil was a native of Yorkshire, a country where, as the Gypsies say, "there's a deadly sight of Bosvils." He was above the middle height, exceedingly strong and active, and one of the best riders in Yorkshire, which is saying a great deal. He was a thorough Gypsy, versed in all the arts of the old race, had two wives, never went to church, and considered that when a man died he was cast into the earth, and there was an end of him. He frequently used to say that if any of his people became Gorgios he would kill them. He had a sister of the name of Clara, a nice, delicate, interesting girl, about fourteen years younger than himself, who travelled about with an aunt; this girl was noticed by a respectable Christian family, who, taking a great interest in her, persuaded her to come and live with them. She was instructed by them in the rudiments of the Christian religion, appeared delighted with her new friends, and promised never to leave them. After the lapse of about six weeks there was a knock at the door; a dark man stood before it who said he wanted Clara. Clara went out trembling, had some discourse with the man in an unknown tongue, and shortly returned in tears, and said that she must go. "What for?" said her friends. "Did you not promise to stay with us?" "I did so," said the girl, weeping more bitterly; "but that man is my brother, who says I must go with him and what he says must be." So with her brother she departed, and her Christian friends never saw her again. What became of her? Was she made away with? Many thought she was, but she was not. Ryley put her into a light cart, drawn by "a flying pony," and hurried her across England, even to distant Norfolk, where he left her, after threatening her, with three Gypsy women who were devoted to him. With these women the writer found her one night encamped in a dark wood, and had much discourse with her, both on Christian and Egyptian matters. She was very melancholy, bitterly regretted having been compelled to quit her Christian friends, and said that she wished she had never been a Gypsy. The writer, after exhorting her to keep a firm grip of her Christianity, departed, and did not see her again for nearly a quarter of a century, when he met her on Epsom Downs, on the Derby day when the terrible horse Gladiateur beat all the English steeds. She was then very much changed, very much changed indeed, appearing as a full-blown Egyptian matron, with two very handsome daughters flaringly dressed in genuine Gypsy fashion, to whom she was giving motherly counsels as to the best means to *hok* and *dukker* the gentlefolks. All her Christianity she appeared to have flung to the dogs, for when the writer spoke to her on that very important subject, she made no answer save by an indescribable Gypsy look. On other matters she was communicative enough, telling the writer, amongst other things, that since he saw her she had been twice married, and both times very well, for that her first husband, by whom she had the two daughters whom the writer "kept staring at," was a man every inch of him, and her second, who was then on the Downs grinding knives with a machine he had, though he had not much manhood, being nearly eighty years old, had something much better, namely a mint of money, which she hoped shortly to have in her own possession.

Ryley, like most of the Bosvils, was a tinker by profession; but, though a tinker, he was amazingly proud and haughty of heart. His grand ambition was to be a great man among his people, a Gypsy King. To this end he furnished himself with clothes made after the costliest Gypsy fashion: the two hinder buttons of the coat, which was of thick blue cloth, were broad gold pieces of Spain, generally called ounces; the fore-buttons were English "spaded guineas"; the buttons of the waistcoat were half-guineas, and those of the collar and the wrists of his shirt were seven-shilling gold pieces. In this coat he would frequently make his appearance on a magnificent horse, whose hoofs, like those of the steed of a Turkish sultan, were cased in shoes of silver. How did he support such expense? it may be asked. Partly by driving a trade in *wafodu luvvu*, counterfeit coin, with which he was supplied by certain honest tradespeople of Brummagem; partly and principally by large sums of money which he received from his two wives, and which they obtained by the practice of certain arts peculiar to Gypsy females. One of his wives was a truly remarkable woman: she was of the Petulengro or Smith tribe; her Christian name, if Christian name it can be called, was Xuri or Shuri, and from her exceeding smartness and cleverness she was generally called by the Gypsies Yocky Shuri, — that is, smart or clever Shuri, *yockey* being a Gypsy word, signifying 'clever.' She could *dukker* — that is, tell fortunes — to perfection, by which alone during the racing season she could make a hundred pounds a month. She was good at the *big hok*, that is, at inducing people to put money into her hands, in the hope of its being multiplied; and, oh dear! how she could *caur* — that is, filch gold rings and trinkets from jewellers cases; the kind of thing which the Spanish Gypsy women called *ustilar pastesas*, filching with the hands. Frequently she would disappear, and travel about England, and Scotland too, *dukkering, hokking*, and *cauring*, and after the lapse of a month return and deliver to her husband, like a true and faithful wife, the proceeds of her industry. So no wonder that the Flying Tinker, as he was called, was enabled to cut a grand appearance. He was very fond of hunting, and would frequently join the field in regular hunting costume, save and except that, instead of the leather hunting-cap, he wore one of fur with a gold band around it, to denote that though he mixed with Gorgios he was still a Romany-chal. Thus equipped and mounted on a capital hunter, whenever he encountered a Gypsy encampment he would invariably dash through it, doing all the harm he could, in order, as he said, to let the *juggals* know that he was their king and had a right to do what he pleased with his own. Things went on swimmingly for a great many years, but, as prosperity does not continue for ever, his dark hour came at last. His wives got into trouble in one or two expeditions, and his dealings in *wafodu luvvu* began to be noised about. Moreover, by his grand airs and violent proceedings he had incurred the hatred of both Gorgios and Gypsies, particularly of the latter, some of whom he had ridden over and lamed for life. One day he addressed his two wives: —

"The Gorgios seek to hang me,
The Gypsies seek to kill me:
This country we must leave."

Shuri.
I'll jaw with you to heaven,
I'll jaw with you to Yaudors —
But not if Lura goes."

Lura.
"I'll jaw with you to heaven,
And to the wicked country,
Though Shuri goeth too."

Ryley.
"Since I must choose betwixt ye,
My choice is Yocky Shuri,
Though Lura loves me best."

Lura.
"My blackest curse on Shuri!
Oh, Ryley, I'll not curse you,
But you will never thrive."

She then took her departure with her cart and donkey, and
Ryley remained with Shuri.

Ryley.
"I've chosen now betwixt ye;
Your wish you now have
        gotten,
But for it you shall smart."

He then struck her with his fist on the cheek, and broke her
jawbone. Shuri uttered no cry or complaint, only mumbled:

"Although with broken jawbone,
I'll follow thee, my Ryley,
Since Lura doesn't jal."

Thereupon Ryley and Yocky Shuri left Yorkshire, and
wended their way to London, where they took up their abode
in the Gypsyry near the Shepherd's Bush. Shuri went about

dukkering and *hokking*, but not with the spirit of former times, for she was not quite so young as she had been, and her jaw, which was never properly cured, pained her much. Ryley went about tinkering, but he was unacquainted with London and its neighbourhood, and did not get much to do. An old Gypsy-man, who was driving about a little cart filled with skewers, saw him standing in a state of perplexity at a place where four roads met.

Old Gypsy.

"Methinks I see a brother!
Who's your father? Who's your mother?
And what may be your name?"

Ryley.

"A Bosvil was my father;
A Bosvil was my mother;
And Ryley is my name."

Old Gypsy.

"I'm glad to see you, brother!
I am a Kaulo Camlo.*
What service can I do?"

Ryley.

"I'm jawing petulengring,†
But do not know the country;
Perhaps you'll show me round."

Old Gypsy.

"I'll sikker tute, prala!
I'm bikkening esconyor;‡
Av, av along with me!"

The old Gypsy showed Ryley about the country for a week or two, and Ryley formed a kind of connection, and did a little business. He, however, displayed little or no energy, was gloomy and dissatisfied, and frequently said that his heart was broken since he had left Yorkshire.

* A Black Lovel.   † Going a-tinkering.
‡ I'll show you about, brother! I'm selling skewers.

Shuri did her best to cheer him, but without effect. Once, when she bade him get up and exert himself, he said that if he did it would be of little use, and asked her whether she did not remember the parting prophecy of his other wife that he would never thrive. At the end of about two years he ceased going his rounds, and did nothing but smoke under the arches of the railroad, and loiter about beershops. At length he became very weak, and took to his bed; doctors were called in by his faithful Shuri, but there is no remedy for a bruised spirit. A Methodist came and asked him, "What was his hope?" "My hope," said he, "is that when I am dead I shall be put into the ground, and my wife and children will weep over me." And such, it may be observed, is the last hope of every genuine Gypsy. His hope was gratified. Shuri and his children, of whom he had three — two stout young fellows and a girl — gave him a magnificent funeral, and screamed, shouted, and wept over his grave. They then returned to the "Arches," not to divide his property amongst them, and to quarrel about the division, according to Christian practice, but to destroy it. They killed his swift pony — still swift, though twenty-seven years of age — and buried it deep in the ground, without depriving it of its skin. They then broke the caravan and cart to pieces, making of the fragments a fire, on which they threw his bedding, carpets, curtains, blankets, and everything which would burn. Finally, they dashed his mirrors, china, and crockery to pieces, hacked his metal pots, dishes and what-not to bits, and flung the whole on the blazing pile. Such was the life, such the death, and such were the funeral obsequies of Ryley Bosvil, a Gypsy who will be long remembered amongst the English Romany for his buttons, his two wives, his grand airs, and last, and not least, for having been the composer of various stanzas in the Gypsy tongue, which have plenty of force, if nothing else, to recommend them. One of these, addressed to Yocky Shuri, runs as follows:

Tuley the Can I kokkeney cam
   Like my rinkeny Yocky Shuri:
Oprey the chongor in ratti I'd cour
   For my rinkeny Yocky Shuri!

Which may be thus rendered:

Beneath the bright sun, there is none, there is none,
  I love like my Yocky Shuri:
With the greatest delight, in blood I would fight
  To the knees for my Yocky Shuri!

Kirk Yetholm

There are two Yetholms — Town Yetholm and Kirk Yetholm. They stand at the distance of about a quarter of a mile from each other, and between them is a valley, down which runs a small stream, called the Beaumont River, crossed by a little stone bridge. Of the town there is not much to be said. It is a long, straggling place, on the road between Morbuttle and Kelso, from which latter place it is distant about seven miles. It is comparatively modern, and sprang up when the Kirk town began to fall into decay. Kirk Yetholm derives the first part of its name from the church, which serves for a place of worship not only for the inhabitants of the place, but for those of the town also. The present church is modern, having been built on the site of the old kirk, which was pulled down in the early part of the present century, and which had been witness of many a strange event connected with the wars between England and Scotland. It stands at the entrance of the place, on the left hand as you turn to the village after ascending the steep road which leads from the bridge. The place occupies the lower portion of a hill, a spur of the Cheviot range, behind which is another hill, much higher, rising to an altitude of at least 900 feet. At one time it was surrounded by a stone wall, and at the farther end is a gateway overlooking a road leading to the English border, from which Kirk Yetholm is distant only a mile and a quarter; the boundary of the two kingdoms being here a small brook called Shorton Burn, on the English side of which is a village of harmless, simple Northumbrians, differing strangely in appearance, manner, and language from the people who live within a stone's throw of them on the other side.

Kirk Yetholm is a small place, but with a remarkable look.

It consists of a street, terminating in what is called a green, with houses on three sides, but open on the fourth, or right side to the mountain, towards which quarter it is grassy and steep. Most of the houses are ancient, and are built of rude stone. By far the most remarkable-looking house is a large and dilapidated building, which has much the appearance of a ruinous Spanish *posada* or *venta*. There is not much life in the place, and you may stand ten minutes where the street opens upon the square without seeing any other human beings than two or three women seated at the house doors, or a ragged, bare-headed boy or two lying on the grass on the upper side of the Green. It came to pass that late one Saturday afternoon, at the commencement of August, in the year 1866, I was standing where the street opens on this Green, or imperfect square. My eyes were fixed on the dilapidated house, the appearance of which awakened in my mind all kinds of odd ideas. "A strange-looking place," said I to myself at last, "and I shouldn't wonder if strange things have been done in it."

"Come to see the Gypsy toon, sir?" said a voice not far from me.

I turned, and saw standing within two yards of me a woman about forty years of age, of decent appearance, though without either cap or bonnet.

"A Gypsy town, is it?" said I; "why, I thought it had been Kirk Yetholm."

Woman. — "Weel, sir, if it is Kirk Yetholm, must it not be a Gypsy toon? Has not Kirk Yetholm ever been a Gypsy toon?"

Myself. — "My good woman, 'ever' is a long term, and Kirk Yetholm must have been Kirk Yetholm long before there were Gypsies in Scotland, or England either."

Woman. — "Weel, sir, your honour may be right, and I dare say is; for your honour seems to be a learned gentleman. Certain, however, it is that Kirk Yetholm has been a Gypsy toon beyond the memory of man."

Myself. — "You do not seem to be a Gypsy."

Woman. — "Seem to be a Gypsy! Na, na, sir! I am the bairn of decent parents, and belong not to Kirk Yetholm, but to Haddington."

Myself. — "And what brought you to Kirk Yetholm?"

Woman. — "Oh, my ain little bit of business brought me to Kirk Yetholm, sir."

Myself. — "Which is no business of mine. That's a queer-looking house there."

Woman. — "The house that your honour was looking at so attentively when I first spoke to ye? A queer-looking house it is, and a queer kind of man once lived in it. Does your honour know who once lived in that house?"

Myself. — "No. How should I? I am here for the first time, and after taking a bite and sup at the inn at the town over yonder I strolled hither."

Woman. — "Does your honour come from far?"

Myself. — "A good way. I came from Strandraar, the farthest part of Galloway, where I landed from a ship which brought me from Ireland."

Woman. — "And what may have brought your honour into these parts?"

Myself. — "Oh, my ain wee bit of business brought me into these parts."

"Which wee bit of business is nae business of mine," said the woman smiling. "Weel, your honour is quite right to keep your ain counsel; for, as your honour weel kens, if a person canna keep his ain counsel it is nae likely that any other body will keep it for him. But to gae back to the queer house, and the queer man that once 'habited it. That man, your honour, was old Will Faa."

Myself. — "Old Will Faa!"

Woman. — "Yes. Old Will Faa, the Gypsy king, smuggler, and innkeeper; he lived in that inn."

Myself. — "Oh, then that house has been an inn?"

Woman. — "It still is an inn, and has always been an inn; and though it has such an eerie look it is sometimes lively enough, more especially after the Gypsies have returned from their summer excursions in the country. It's a roaring place then. They spend most of their sleight-o'-hand gains in that house."

Myself. — "Is the house still kept by a Faa?"

Woman. — "No, sir; there are no Faas to keep it. The name is clean dead in the land, though there is still some of the blood remaining."

Myself. — "I really should like to see some of the blood."

Woman. — "Weel, sir, you can do that without much difficulty; there are not many Gypsies just now in Kirk Yetholm; but the one who they say has more of his blood than any one else happens to be here. I mean his grandbairn — his daughter's daughter; she whom they ca' the 'Gypsy Queen o' Yetholm,' and whom they lead about the toon once a year, mounted on a cuddy, with a tin crown on her head, with much shouting, and with mony a barbaric ceremony."

Myself. — "I really should like to see her."

Woman. — "Weel, sir, there's a woman behind you, seated at the doorway, who can get your honour not only the sight of her, but the speech of her, for she is one of the race, and a relation of hers; and, to tell ye the truth, she has had her eye upon your honour for some time past expecting to be asked about the queen, for scarcely anybody comes to Yetholm but goes to see the queen; and some gae so far as to say that they merely crowned her queen in hopes of bringing grist to the Gypsy mill."

I thanked the woman, and was about to turn away, in order to address myself to the other woman seated on the step, when my obliging friend said, "I beg your pardon, sir, but before ye go I wish to caution you, when you get to the speech of the queen, not to put any speerings to her about a certain tongue or dialect which they say the Gypsies have. All the Gypsies become glum and dour as soon as they are spoken to about their language, and particularly the queen. The queen might say something uncivil to your honour, should you ask her questions about her language."

Myself. — "Oh, then the Gypsies of Yetholm have a language of their own?"

Woman. — "I canna say, sir; I dinna ken whether they have or not; I have been at Yetholm several years, about my ain wee bit o' business, and never heard them utter a word that was not either English or broad Scotch. Some people say that they have a language of their ain, and others say that they have nane, and moreover that, though they call themselves Gypsies, they are far less Gypsy than Irish, a great deal of Irish being mixed in their veins with a very little of the much more respectable Gypsy blood. It may be sae, or it may be not; perhaps your honour will find out. That's the woman, sir, just behind the door. Gud e'en. I maun noo gang and boil my cup o'tay."

To the woman at the door I now betook myself. She was seated on the threshold, and employed in knitting. She was dressed in white, and had a cap on her head, from which depended a copule of ribbons, one on each side. As I drew near she looked up. She had a full, round, smooth face, and her complexion was brown, or rather olive, a hue which contrasted with that of her eyes, which were blue.

"There is something Gypsy in that face," said I to myself, as I looked at her; "but I don't like those eyes."

"A fine evening," said I to her at last.

"Yes, sir," said the woman, with very little of the Scotch accent; "it is a fine evening. Come to see the town?"

"Yes," said I; "I am come to see the town. A nice little town it seems."

"And I suppose come to see the Gypsies, too," said the woman, with a half smile.

"Well," said I, "to be frank with you, I came to see the Gypsies. You are not one, I suppose?"

"Indeed I am," said the woman, rather sharply, "and who shall say that I am not, seeing that I am a relation of old Will Faa, the man whom the woman from Haddington was speaking to you about; for I heard her mention his name?"

"Then," said I, "you must be related to her whom they call the Gypsy queen."

"I am, indeed, sir. Would you wish to see her?"

"By all means," said I. "I should wish very much to see the Gypsy queen."

"Then I will show you to her, sir; many gentlefolks from England come to see the Gypsy queen of Yetholm. Follow me, sir!"

She got up, and, without laying down her knitting-work, went round the corner, and began to ascend the hill. She was strongly made, and was rather above the middle height. She conducted me to a small house, some little way up the hill. As we were going, I said to her, "As you are a Gypsy, I suppose you have no objection to a *coro* of *koshto levinor?*"*

* A cup of good ale.

She stopped her knitting for a moment, and appeared to consider, and then resuming it, she said hesitatingly, "No, sir, no! None at all. That is, not exactly!"

"She is no true Gypsy, after all," said I to myself.

We went through a little garden to the door of the house, which stood ajar. She pushed it open and looked in; then, turning round, she said: "She is not here, sir; but she is close at hand. Wait here till I go and fetch her." She went to a house a little farther up the hill, and I presently saw her returning with another female, of slighter build, lower in stature, and apparently much older. She came towards me with much smiling, smirking, and nodding, which I returned with as much smiling and nodding as if I had known her for threescore years. She motioned me with her hand to enter the house. I did so. The other woman returned down the hill, and the queen of the Gypsies entering, and shutting the door, confronted me on the floor, and said, in a rather musical, but slightly faltering voice:

"Now, sir, in what can I oblige you?"

Thereupon, letting the umbrella fall, which I invariably carry about with me in my journeyings, I flung my arms three times up into the air, and in an exceedingly disagreeable voice, owing to a cold which I had had for some time, and which I had caught amongst the lakes of Loughmaben, whilst hunting after Gypsies whom I could not find, I exclaimed:

"Sossi your nav? Pukker mande tute's nav! Shan tu a mumpli-mushi, or a tatchi Romany?"

Which, interpreted into Gorgio, runs thus:

"What is your name? Tell me your name! Are you a mumping woman, or a true Gypsy?"

The woman appeared frightened, and for some time said nothing, but only stared at me. At length, recovering herself, she exclaimed, in an angry tone, "Why do you talk to me in that manner, and in that gibberish? I don't understand a word of it."

"Gibberish!" said I; "it is no gibberish; it is Zingarrijib, Romany rokrapen, real Gypsy of the old order."

"Whatever it is," said the woman, "it's of no use speaking it to me. If you want to speak to me, you must speak English or Scotch."

"Why, they told me as how you were a Gypsy," said I.

169

"And they told you the truth," said the woman; "I am a Gypsy, and a real one; I am not ashamed of my blood."

"If yer were a Gyptian," said I, "yer would be able to speak Gyptian; but yer can't, not a word."

"At any rate," said the woman, "I can speak English, which is more than you can. Why, your way of speaking is that of the lowest vagrants of the roads."

"Oh, I have two or three ways of speaking English," said I; "and when I speaks to low wagram folks, I speaks in a low wagram manner."

"Not very civil," said the woman.

"A pretty Gypsy!" said I; "why, I'll be bound you don't know what a *churi* is!"

The woman gave me a sharp look; but made no reply.

"A pretty queen of the Gypsies!" said I; "why, she doesn't know the meaning of *churi*!"

"Doesn't she?" said the woman, evidently nettled; "doesn't she?"

"Why, do you mean to say that you know the meaning of *churi*?"

"Why, of course I do," said the woman.

"Hardly, my good lady," said I; "hardly; a *churi* to you is merely a *churi*."

"A *churi* is a knife," said the woman, in a tone of defiance; "a *churi* is a knife."

"Oh, it is," said I; "and yet you tried to persuade me that you had no peculiar language of your own, and only knew English and Scotch: *churi* is a word of the language in which I spoke to you at first, Zingarrijib, or Gypsy language; and since you know that word, I make no doubt that you know others, and in fact can speak Gypsy. Come; let us have a little confidential discourse together."

The woman stood for some time, as if in reflection, and at length said: "Sir, before having any particular discourse with you, I wish to put a few questions to you, in order to gather from your answers whether it is safe to talk to you on Gypsy matters. You pretend to understand the Gypsy language: if I find you do not, I will hold no further discourse with you; and the sooner you take yourself off the better. If I find you do, I will talk with you as long as you like. What do you call that?" — and she pointed to the fire.

"Speaking Gyptianly?" said I.

The woman nodded.

"Whoy, I calls that *yog*."

"Hm," said the woman: "and the dog out there?"

"Gyptian-loike?" said I.

"Yes."

"Whoy, I calls that a *juggal*."

"And the hat on your head?"

"Well, I have two words for that: a *staury* and a *stadge*."

"*Stadge*," said the woman, "we call it here. Now what's a gun?"

"There is no Gypsy in England," said I, "can tell you the word for a gun; at least the proper word, which is lost. They have a word — *yag-engro* — but that is a made-up word signifying a fire-thing."

"Then you don't know the word for a gun," said the Gypsy.

"Oh dear me! Yes," said I; "the genuine Gypsy word for a gun is *puschca*. But I did not pick up that word in England, but in Hungary, where the Gypsies retain their language better than in England: *puschca* is the proper word for a gun, and not *yag-engro*, which may mean a fire-shovel, tongs, poker, or anything connected with fire, quite as well as a gun."

"*Puschca* is the word, sure enough," said the Gypsy. "I thought I should have caught you there; and now I have but one more question to ask you, and when I have done so, you may as well go; for I am quite sure you cannot answer it. What is *Nokkum*?"

"*Nokkum*," said I; "*nokkum*?"

"Aye," said the Gypsy; "what is *Nokkum*? Our people here, besides their common name of Romany, have a private name for themselves, which is *Nokkum* or *Nokkums*. Why do the children of the Caungri Foros call themselves *Nokkums*?"

"*Nokkum*," said I; "*nokkum*? The root of *nokkum* must be *nok*, which signifieth a nose."

"A—h!" said the Gypsy, slowly drawing out the monosyllable, as if in astonishment.

"Yes," said I: "the root of *nokkum* is assuredly *nok*, and I have no doubt that your people call themselves *Nokkum* because they are in the habit of *nosing* the Gorgios. *Nokkums* means *Nosems*."

"Sit down, sir," said the Gypsy, handing me a chair. "I am now ready to talk to you as much as you please about *Nokkum* words and matters, for I see there is no danger. But I tell you frankly that had I not found that you knew as much as, or a great deal more than, myself, not a hundred pounds, nor indeed all the money in Berwick, should have induced me to hold discourse with you about the words and matters of the Brown children of Kirk Yetholm."

I sat down in the chair which she handed me; she sat down in another, and we were presently in deep discourse about matters *Nokkum*. We first began to talk about words, and I soon found that her knowledge of Romany was anything but extensive; far less so, indeed, than that of the commonest English Gypsy woman, for whenever I addressed her in regular Gypsy sentences, and not in *poggado jib*, or broken language, she would giggle and say I was too deep for her. I should say that the sum total of her vocabulary barely amounted to three hundred words. Even of these there were several which were not pure Gypsy words — that is, belonging to the speech which the ancient Zingary brought with them to Britain. Some of her bastard Gypsy words belonged to the cant or allegorical jargon of thieves, who, in order to disguise their real meaning, call one thing by the name of another. For example, she called a shilling a 'hog,' a word belonging to the old English cant dialect, instead of calling it by the genuine Gypsy term *tringurushi*, the literal meaning of which is three groats. Then she called a donkey 'asal,' and a stone 'cloch,' which words are neither cant nor Gypsy, but Irish or Gaelic. I incurred her vehement indignation by saying they were Gaelic. She contradicted me flatly, and said that whatever else I might know I was quite wrong there; for that neither she nor any one of her people would condescend to speak anything so low as Gaelic, or indeed, if they possibly could avoid it, to have anything to do with the poverty-stricken creatures who used it. It is a singular fact that, though principally owing to the magic writings of Walter Scott, the Highland Gael and Gaelic have obtained the highest reputation in every other part of the world, they are held in the Lowlands in very considerable contempt. There the Highlander, elsewhere "the bold Gael with sword and buckler," is the type of poverty and wretchedness; and his

172

language, elsewhere "the fine old Gaelic, the speech of Adam and Eve in Paradise," is the designation of every unintelligible jargon. But not to digress. On my expressing to the Gypsy queen my regret that she was unable to hold with me a regular conversation in Romany, she said that no one regretted it more than herself, but that there was no help for it; and that slight as I might consider her knowledge of Romany to be, it was far greater than that of any other Gypsy on the Border, or indeed in the whole of Scotland; and that as for the *Nokkums*, there was not one on the Green who was acquainted with half a dozen words of Romany, though the few words they had they prized high enough, and would rather part with their heart's blood than communicate them to a stranger.

"Unless," said I, "they found the stranger knew more than themselves."

"That would make no difference with them," said the queen, "though it has made a great deal of difference with me. They would merely turn up their noses, and say they had no Gaelic. You would not find them so communicative as me; the *Nokkums*, in general, are a dour set, sir."

Before quitting the subject of language it is but right to say that though she did not know much Gypsy, and used cant and Gaelic terms, she possessed several words unknown to the English Romany, but which are of the true Gypsy order. Amongst them was the word *tirrehi*, or *tirrehai*, signifying shoes or boots, which I had heard in Spain and in the east of Europe. Another was *calches* a Wallachian word signifying trousers. Moreover, she gave the right pronunciation to the word which denotes a man not of Gypsy blood, saying *gajo*, and not *gorgio*, as the English Gypsies do. After all, her knowledge of Gentle Romany was not altogether to be sneezed at.

Ceasing to talk to her about words, I began to question her about the Faas. She said that a great number of the Faas had come in the old time to Yetholm, and settled down there, and that her own forefathers had always been the principal people among them. I asked her if she remembered her grandfather, old Will Faa, and received for answer that she remembered him very well, and that I put her very much in mind of him, being a tall, lusty man, like himself, and having a skellying look with the left eye, just like him. I asked her if she had not seen queer folks at Yetholm in her grandfather's time. "*Dosta dosta*," said she; "plenty, plenty of queer folk I saw at Yetholm in my grandfather's time, and plenty I have seen since, and not the least queer is he who is now asking me questions." "Did you ever see Piper Allen?" said I; "he was a great friend of your grandfather's." "I never saw him," she replied; "but I have often heard of him. He married one of our people." "He did so," said I, "and the marriage-feast was held on the Green just behind us. He got a good, clever wife, and she got a bad, rascally husband. One night, after taking an affectionate farewell of her, he left her on an expedition, with plenty of money in his pocket, which he had obtained from her, and which she had procured by her dexterity. After going about four miles he bethought himself that she had still some money, and returning crept up to the room in which she lay asleep, and stole her pocket, in which were eight guineas; then slunk away, and never returned, leaving her in poverty, from which she never recovered." I then mentioned Madge Gordon, at one time the Gypsy queen of the Border, who used, magnificently dressed, to ride about on a pony shod with silver, inquiring if she had ever seen her. She said she had frequently seen Madge Faa, for that was her name, and not Gordon; but that when she knew her, all her magnificence, beauty, and royalty had left her; for she was then a poor, poverty-stricken old woman, just able with a pipkin in her hand to totter to the well on the Green for water. Then with much nodding, winking, and skellying, I began to talk about *Drabbing bawlor, dooking gryes, cauring*, and *hokking*, and asked if them'ere things were ever done by the *Nokkums*: and received for answer that she believed such things were occasionally done, not by the *Nokkums*, but by other Gypsies, with whom her people had no connection.

Observing her eyeing me rather suspiciously, I changed the subject; asking her if she had travelled much about. She told me she had, and that she had visited most parts of Scotland, and seen a good bit of the northern part of England.

"Did you travel alone?" said I.

"No," said she; "when I travelled in Scotland I was with some of my own people, and in England with the Lees and Bosvils."

'Old acquaintances of mine," said I; "why only the other day I was with them at Fairlop Fair, in the Wesh."

"I frequently heard them talking of Epping Forest," said the Gypsy; "a nice place, is it not?"

"The loveliest forest in the world!" said I. "Not equal to what it was, but still the loveliest forest in the world, and the pleasantest, especially in summer; for then it is thronged with grand company, and the nightingales, and cuckoos, and Romany *chals* and *chies*. As for Romany-chals there is not such a place for them in the whole world as the Forest. Them that wants to see Romany-chals should go to the Forest, especially to the Bald-faced Hind on the hill above Fairlop, on the day of Fairlop Fair. It is their trysting-place, as you would say, and there they musters from all parts of England, and there they whoops, dances, and plays; keeping some order nevertheless, because the *Rye* of all the Romans is in the house, seated behind the door: —

> Romany Chalor
> Anglo the wuddur
> Mistos are boshing;
> Mande beshello
> Innar the wuddur
> Shooning the boshipen."

> *Roman lads*
> *Before the door*
> *Bravely fiddle;*
> *Here I sit*
> *Within the door*
> *And hear them fiddle.*

"I wish I knew as much Romany as you, sir," said the Gypsy. "Why, I never heard so much Romany before in all my life."

She was rather a small woman, apparently between sixty and seventy, with intelligent and rather delicate features. Her complexion was darker than that of the other female; but she had the same kind of blue eyes. The room in which we were seated was rather long, and tolerably high. In the wall, on the side which fronted the windows which looked out upon the

175

Green, were oblong holes for beds, like those seen in the sides of a cabin. There was nothing of squalor or poverty about the place.

Wishing to know her age, I inquired of her what it was. She looked angry, and said she did not know.

"Are you forty-nine?" said I, with a terrible voice, and a yet more terrible look.

"More," said she, with a smile; "I am sixty-eight."

There was something of the gentlewoman in her: on my offering her money she refused to take it, saying that she did not want it, and it was with the utmost difficulty that I persuaded her to accept a trifle, with which, she said, she would buy herself some tea.

But withal there was *hukni* in her, and by that she proved her Gypsy blood. I asked her if she would be at home on the following day, for in that case I would call and have some more talk with her, and received for answer that she would be at home and delighted to see me. On going, however, on the following day, which was Sunday, I found the garden-gate locked and the window-shutters up, plainly denoting that there was nobody at home.

Seeing some men lying on the hill, a little way above, who appeared to be observing me, I went up to them for the purpose of making inquiries. They were all the young men, and decently though coarsely dressed. None wore the Scottish cap or bonnet, but all the hat of England. Their countenances were rather dark, but had nothing of the vivacious expression observable in the Gypsy face, but much of the dogged, sullen look which makes the countenances of the generality of the Irish who inhabit London and some other of the large English towns so disagreeable. They were lying on their bellies, occasionally kicking their heels into the air. I greeted them civilly, but received no salutation in return.

"Is So-and-so at home?" said I.

"No," said one, who, though seemingly the eldest of the party, could not have been more than three-and-twenty years of age; "she is gone out."

"Is she gone far?" said I.

"No," said the speaker, kicking up his heels.

"Where is she gone to?"

"She's gone to Cauldstrame."

"How far is that?"

"Just thirteen miles."

"Will she be at home to-day?"

"She may, or she may not."

"Are you of her people?" said I.

"No—h," said the fellow, slowly drawing out the word.

"Can you speak Irish?"

"No—h; I can't speak Irish," said the fellow, tossing up his nose, and then flinging up his heels.

"You know what *arragod* is?" said I.

"No—h!"

"But you know what *ruppy* is?" said I; and thereupon I winked and nodded.

"No—h;" and then up went the nose, and subsequently the heels.

"Good day," said I; and turned away; I received no counter-salutation; but, as I went down the hill, there was none of the shouting and laughter which generally follow a discomfited party. They were a hard, sullen, cautious set, in whom a few drops of Gypsy blood were mixed with some Scottish and a much larger quantity of low Irish. Between them and their queen a striking difference was observable. In her there was both fun and cordiality; in them not the slightest appearance of either. What was the cause of this disparity? The reason was they were neither the children nor the grandchildren of real Gypsies, but only the remote descendants, whereas she was the granddaughter of two genuine Gypsies, old Will Faa and his wife, whose daughter was her mother; so that she might be considered all but a thorough Gypsy; for being by her mother's side a Gypsy, she was of course much more so than she would have been had she sprung from a Gypsy father and a Gentile mother; the qualities of a child, both mental and bodily, depending much less on the father than on the mother. Had her father been a Faa, instead of her mother, I should probably never have heard from her lips a single word of Romany, but found her as sullen and inductile as the *Nokkums* on the Green, whom it was of little more use questioning than so many stones.

Nevertheless, she had played me the *hukni*, and that was not very agreeable; so I determined to be even with her, and by some means or other to see her again. Hearing that on the

177

next day, which was Monday, a great fair was to be held in the neighbourhood of Kelso, I determined to go thither, knowing that the likeliest place in all the world to find a Gypsy at is a fair; so I went to the grand cattle-fair of St. George, held near the ruined castle of Roxburgh, in a lovely meadow not far from the juuction of the Teviot and Tweed; and there sure enough, on my third saunter up and down, I met my Gypsy. We met in the most cordial manner — smirks and giggling on her side, smiles and nodding on mine. She was dressed respectably in black, and was holding the arm of a stout wench, dressed in garments of the same colour, who she said was her neice, and a *rinkeni rakli*. The girl whom she called *rinkeni* or handsome, but whom I did not consider handsome, had much of the appearance of one of those *Irish* girls, born in London, whom one so frequently sees carrying milk-pails about the streets of the metropolis. By the bye, how is it that the children born in England of Irish parents account themselves Irish and not English, whilst the children born in Ireland of English parents call themselves not English but Irish? Is it because there is ten times more nationality in Irish blood than in English? After the smirks, smiles, and salutations were over, I inquired whether there were many Gypsies in the fair. "Plenty," said she, "plenty Tates, Andersons, Reeds, and many others. That woman is an Anderson — yonder is a Tate," said she, pointing to two common-looking females. "Have they much Romany?" said I. "No," said she, "scarcely a word." "I think I shall go and speak to them," said I. "Don't," said she; "they would only be uncivil to you. Moreover, they have nothing of that kind — on the word of a *rawnie* they have not."

I looked in her eyes; there was nothing of *hukni* in them, so I shook her by the hand; and through rain and mist, for the day was a wretched one, trudged away to Dryburgh to pay my respects at the tomb of Walter Scott, a man with whose principles I have no sympathy, but for whose genius I have always entertained the most intense admiration.

THE END

Stock List

Rpr. 1937 = Reprinted 1937 edition
N. Intro. = New Introduction by. Ed. = Edited by
All books are sewn case bound unless marked *paper*.

Avalon and Sedgemoor. Desmond Hawkins.
ISBN 0 86299 016 5. 192pp illustrated. 219mm × 157mm.
£4.50, $9.50. *Paper edition only.*

Along the Great North and Other Roads,
The North Road Cycling Club 1885–1980. A.B. Smith.
ISBN 904387 73 9. 192pp. 219mm × 157mm. £6.95, $15.75

Canonical Houses of Wells. Sherwin Bailey.
ISBN 0 904387 91 7. 192pp. 215mm × 138mm.
£8.95, $18.75.

In Chimley Corner. Jan Stewer. Rpr. 1927. ISBN
0 904387 56 9. 256pp. 196mm × 127mm £4.95. $11.25

Chronicles of London. C.L. Kingsford. Rpr. 1905.
ISBN 0 904387 15 1. x.viii + 368pp. 216mm × 138mm.
£14.00. Not available from Humanities Press.

**The Civil War in Worcestershire, 1642-1646; and the
Scotch Invasion of 1651.** J.W. Willis-Bund. Rpr. 1905,
ISBN 0 904387 32 1. vi + 268p. 4pp illus. 3pp maps.
216mm × 138mm. £6.95, $15.75.

The Complete Peerage. George Edward Cockayne et al.
ISBN 0 904387 82 8. 6 vols. Photoreduced 4pp to view
472pp, 584pp, 408pp, 496pp, 448pp, 416pp.
248mm × 172mm. £300.00, $675.00.

Concerning Agnes. Desmond Hawkins.
ISBN 0 904387 97 6. 160pp illustrated. 235mm × 155mm.
£7.95, $16.75.

Cotswold Churches. David Verey. ISBN 0 904387 78 X.
192pp illustrated. 219mm × 157mm. £3.95, $9.00.
Paper edition only.

A Cotteswold Manor, being the History of Painswick.
Welbore St. Clair Baddeley. Rpr. 1929. N. Intro.
Geoffrey Saunders. ISBN 0 904387 54 2. xiv + 262pp.
42pp ilus. 219mm 157mm. £12.00, $27.00.

The Crown and Local Communities in England and
France in the Fifteenth Century. Ed. J.R.L. Highfield &
Robin Jeffs. ISBN 0 904387 67 4. 192pp. 219mm × 157mm.
£8.95, $11.25. *Paper* ISBN 0 904387 79 8. £4.95, $11.25

The Diary of a Cotswold Parson. Revd. F.E. Witts,
1783-1854. Ed. David Verey. ISBN 0 904387 19 4.
192pp illustrated. 216mm × 138mm. £7.95, $19.25.
Paper ISBN 0 904387 33 X. £3.95, $8.00.

The Diary of a Pilgrimage. Jerome K. Jerome.
ISBN 0 86299 010 6. 160pp illustrated. 192mm × 127mm.
£1.95, $4.25. *Paper edition only.*

The Diary of a Rowing Tour from Oxford to London in
1875. Howard Williams. ISBN 0 904387 69 0.
168pp illustrated. 219mm × 157mm. £7.95, $16.75.
Paper ISBN 0 904387 74 4. £3.95, $8.25.

Dursley and Cam. David E. Evans. ISBN 0 904387 88 7.
128pp illustrated. 219mm × 157mm. £3.95, $8.25.
Paper edition only.

The English Landscape Garden. H.F. Clark. Rpr. 1948.
ISBN 0 904387 38 0. 96pp + 32pp illus.
248mm × 172mm. £6.00, $16.50.

Evergreens and Other Short Stories. Jerome K. Jerome.
ISBN 0 86299 011 4. 112pp illustrated 192mm × 124mm.
£1.50, $3.25.

Excellent Cassandra. Joan Johnson. ISBN 0 904387 76 3.
160pp illustrated. 219mm × 157mm. £7.95, $18.00.

**False, Fleeting, Perjur'd Clarence, George, Duke of
Clarence 1449–78.** Michael Hicks. ISBN 0 904387 44 5.
270pp. 8pp illus. 216mm × 138mm. £8.95, $20.00.

Frederick III, German Emperor 1888. John Van der Kiste.
ISBN 0 904387 77 1. 244pp illustrated. 219mm × 157mm.
£8.95, $20.25.

George Thorpe and the Berkeley Company.
Eric Gethyn-Jones. ISBN 0 904387 83 6. 296pp
illustrated. 219mm × 157mm. £7.95, $18.00.

Gloucester Cathedral. David Verey & David Welander.
ISBN 0 904387 40 2. £6.95, $15.75. 160pp illustrated.
219mm × 157mm. *Paper* ISBN 0 904387 34 8. £3.95, $8.00.

Gloucestershire Churches. David Verey. ISBN 0 904387
78 X. 192pp illustrated (32pp full colour).
245mm × 169mm. £12.95, $6.75. *Paper edition only.*

A Handful of History. J.R.S. Whiting.
ISBN 0 86299 0002 9. vi + 201pp illustrated.
230mm × 154mm. £4.25, $9.00.

Historical Records of Bisley with Lypiatt.
Mary A. Rudd. Rpr. 1937. N. Intro. Geoffrey Sanders.
ISBN 0 904387 16 X. xii + 438pp. 16pp illus.
216mm × 138mm. £11.00, $24.75.

A History of Cheltenham. Gwen Hart.
ISBN 0 904387 87 9. 350pp illustrated (col. frontis.).
219mm × 157mm. £12.50, $26.25.

History of Cirencester, The Roman Corinium.
K.J. Beecham. Rpr. 1887 + additions booklet 1910. N.
Intro. David Verey. ISBN 0 904387 18 6. vi + 314 +
30pp illustrated. 200mm × 235mm. £11.00, $24.75.

A History of Malvern. Brian S. Smith.
ISBN 0 904387 31 3. x + 310pp illustrated.
216mm × 138mm. £6.50, $14.75.

The History of King Richard the Third.
Sir George Buck. Ed. A.N. Kincaid. ISBN 0 904387 26 7.
cxlvi + 362pp. 225mm × 172mm. £30.00, $60.50.
Paper ISBN 0 86299 008 4. £16.00, $34.00.

A History of Tetbury. Eric Hodgson.
ISBN 0 904387 10 0. 136pp. 32pp illus.
216mm × 138mm. £6.95, $15.75.

A House of Correction. J.R.S. Whiting.
ISBN 0 904387 27 5. 124pp illustrated.
216mm × 138mm. £5.50, $12.50.

Idle Thoughts of an Idle Fellow. Jerome K. Jerome.
ISBN 0 86299 009 2. 144pp illustrated. 192mm × 124mm.
£1.95, $4.25.

Illustrated Cheltenham Guide of 1845. George Rowe.
ISBN 0 904387 95 X. 168pp illustrated. 216mm × 157mm.
£3.95, $8.25. *Paper edition only.*

The Ingenious Mr. Pedersen. David E. Evans.
ISBN 0 904387 29 1. 128pp illustrated. 216mm × 138mm.
£4.50, $10.25.

In Spite of Dungeons. S.J. Davies. ISBN 0 904387 11 9.
192pp illustrated. 216mm × 138mm. *Paper.* £3.95, $7.50.

Letters from a Flying Officer. Rothesay Stuart Wortley.
ISBN 0 86299 17 3. viii + 208pp illustrated.
192mm × 127mm. £3.95, $8.25. *Paper edition only.*

Lister's — The First Hundred Years. David E. Evans.
ISBN 0 904387 23 2. 256pp illustrated. 216mm × 138mm.
£6.95, $15.75.

Men and Armour for Gloucestershire in 1608.
John Smith. Rpr. 1902. ISBN 0 904387 49 6. xiv + 424pp.
248mm × 172mm. £20.00, $36.00.

Methodism and the Revolt of the Field. Nigel Scotland.
ISBN 0 904387 46 1. 296pp illustrated. 219mm × 157mm.
£12.00, $22.50.

Minchinhampton and Avening. A.T. Playne. Rpr. 1915.
N. Intro. Geoffrey Sanders. ISBN 0 904387 25 9.
xii + 188pp. 24pp illus. 216mm × 138mm. £9.00, $20.50.

A Month in England. H.T. Tuckerman.
ISBN 0 86299 020 3. 156pp illustrated. 192mm × 124mm.
£2.95, $6.25.

Moonraker County. Lornie Leete-Hodge.
ISBN 0 904387 92 5. 144pp illustrated. 219mm × 157mm.
£3.95. *Paper edition only.* Not available in U.S.A.

An Account of the Mutiny on HMS Bounty.
William Bligh. Ed. Robert Bowman. ISBN 0 904387 47 X.
160pp illustrated. 248mm × 172mm. £8.95, $23.50.
Paper ISBN 0 86299 005 X. £4.95, $10.50.

The Mystery of the Princes. Audrey Williamson.
ISBN 0 904387 28 3. 216pp. 16pp illus. 216mm × 138mm.
£6.95. *Paper* ISBN 0 904387 48 8. £3.95, $8.25.
Paper edition only available from Humanities Press.

John Nash and the Village Picturesque. Nigel Temple.
ISBN 0 904387 24 0. xx + 176pp. 32pp illus.
248mm × 172mm. £15.00, $33.00.
Paper ISBN 0 86299 007 6. £5.95, $12.50.

The Old Gloucester, The Story of a Cattle Breed.
Adam Stout. ISBN 0 904387 42 9. 96pp. 10pp illus.
3 maps. 216mm × 138mm £4.95, $11.25

A Parcel of Ol' Crams. Jan Stewer. Rpr. 1930.
ISBN 0 904387 57 7. 256pp. 196mm × 127mm. £4.95,
$11.25.

Patronage the Crown and the Provinces in Later
Medieval England. Ed. Ralph A. Griffiths. ISBN
0 904387 43 3. 192pp. 219mm × 157mm. £7.95, $20.75.

**Patronage Pedigree and Power in Later Medieval
England.** Ed. Charles Ross. ISBN 0 904387 37 2. 224pp.
216mm × 138mm. £7.95. Not available from Humanities
Press.

**Richard III as Duke of Gloucester and King of
England.** Caroline A. Halsted. Rpr. 1844.
ISBN 0 904387 14 3. 2 vols., xiv + 458pp, xii + 602pp.
216mm × 138mm. £30.00, $67.50.
Paper ISBN 0 904387 41 0. £16.00, $36.00.

Richard III up to Shakespeare. George E. Churchill.
Rpr. 1900. ISBN 904387 05 4. 548pp. 216mm. × 138mm.
£12.00. Not available from Humanities Press.

Roman Gloucestershire. Alan McWhirr.
ISBN 0 904387 63 1. 192pp illustrated. 219mm × 157mm.
£7.95, $18.00. *Paper* ISBN 0 904387 60 7. £3.95, $9.00.

Roman Mosaics in Britain. David Neal.
ISBN 0 904387 64 X. 208pp illustrated. + 4pp full colour.
Volume includes 2 colour microfiche. 297mm × 210mm.
£9.95, $22.50. *Paper edition only.*

Romano-Lavo-Lil, A Book of the Gypsy. George Borrow.
ISBN 0 86299 024 6. 192pp. 192mm × 124mm.
£2.95, £6.25.

The Rous Roll. John Rous. Rpr. 1859. N. Intro
Charles Ross. ISBN 0 904387 43 7. xviii + 134p
32pp illus. 248mm × 172mm. £12.00, $31.50

The Rural Economy of Glocestershire. William N
Rpr. 1796. ISBN 0 904387 22 4. vols., xxxii +
xxiv + 368pp. 200 × 130mm. £28.00, $54.00. (2 v

Somersetshire Delineated. C. & J. Greenwood. R
N. Intro. Robert Dunning. ISBN 0 904387 54 4
viii + 216pp. 216mm × 138mm. £6.95, $13.50.

Southern History volume 3. Ed. J.R. Lowerson
ISBN 0 904387 65 8. 288pp. 216mm × 138mm.
$28.25.*Paper* ISBN 0 904387 66 6. £7.50, $17.0
Volume 4. Ed. J.R. Lowerson. ISBN 0 904387
296pp. 216mm × 138mm. £12.50, $28.25.
Paper ISBN 0 904387 94 1. £7.50, $17.00.

Stow-on-the-Wold. Joan Johnson. ISBN 0 9043
160pp. 19pp illus. 3 maps. 216mm × 138mm. £6.95

The Stroudwater Canal. Michael Handford.
ISBN 0 904387 30 5. 337pp. + 32pp illus.
216mm × 138mm. £8.95, $21.25. Paper £4.95,

Three Men in a Boat. Jerome K. Jerome.
ISBN 0 86299 028 9. 240pp illustrated. 192mm ×
£1.95, $4.25.

Three Men on the Bummel. Jerome K. Jerom
ISBN 0 86299 029 7. 232pp illustrated. 192mm ×
£1.95, $4.25.

Under the Hill. Simon Herrick ISBN 0 904387
144pp illustrated. 219mm × 157mm. £4.95, $11

A Voyage to New Holland. William Dampier.
James Spencer. ISBN 904387 75 5. 256pp illust
248mm × 172mm. £9.95, $22.50.

Wall Painting in Roman Britain. Norman D
Roger Ling. ISBN 904387 96 8. 232pp illustrate
(+ 8pp full colour). Volume includes 1 colour m
297mm × 210mm. £11.95, $25.25. *Paper editio*

West Country Gardens. John Sales. ISBN 0 904
272pp. 15pp illus. 4pp full colour. 13 maps.
216mm × 154mm. £7.95, $18.00.
Paper ISBN 0 904387 84 4. £3.95, $8.25.

West Midland Gardens. Ron Sidwell.
ISBN 0 904387 71 2. 256pp illustrated (8pp full
219mm × 157mm. £7.95, $18.00.

White Horses and other Hill Figures. Morris
ISBN 0 904387 59 3. 224pp illustrated. 216mm ×
£3.95, $9.00. *Paper edition only.*

In a Wiltshire Village. Scenes from Rural Victo
Alfred Williams. Ed. Michael J. Davis.
ISBN 0 904387 62 3. 192pp illustrated. 219mm ×
£3.95, $9.00. *Paper edition only.*

The Witchcraft and Folklore of Dartmoor.
Ruth St Leger-Gordon. ISBN 0 86299 021 1. 1
illustrated. 219mm × 157mm. £3.95, $9.00.
Paper edition only.

Wotton-under-Edge. E.S. Lindley. ISBN 0 904
344pp. 16pp illus. 216mm × 138mm. £7.50, $1

Wotton-under-Edge, A Century of Change.
Geoffrey Masefield. ISBN 0 904387 51 8. 112p
52pp illus. 219mm × 145mm. £3.95, $9.00.
Paper edition only